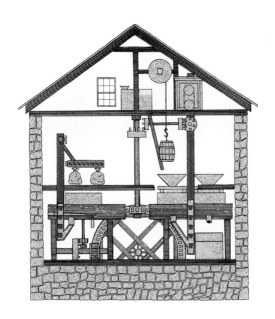

Mill

Mill

The History and Future of Naturally Powered Buildings

David Larkin

with principal photography by Paul Rocheleau

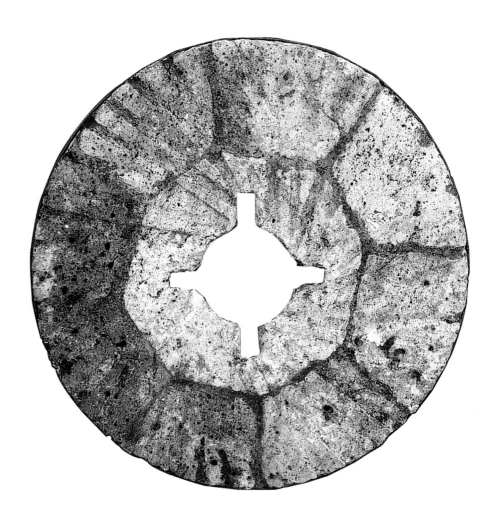

A DAVID LARKIN BOOK
Universe Publishing

Universe Editor: Richard Olsen
Copy Editor: Iris Becker
Production: Belinda Hellinger

First published in the United States of America in 2000
By UNIVERSE PUBLISHING
A Division of Rizzoli International Publications, Inc.
300 Park Avenue South
New York, NY 10010

Librari of Congress Cataloging-in-Publication Data
   Mill: the history and future of naturally powered buildings/David Larkin; principal
photography by Paul Rocheleau.
     p. cm.
   ISBN 0-7893-0501-1
   1. Windmills--History. 2. Water mills--History. I. Rocheleau, Paul. II. Title.
TJ823 .L36 2000   00-044350
725'.4--dc21

00 01 02 03 / 10 9 8 7 6 5 4 3 2 1

Printed in Italy

Contents

Introduction 6

The Country Miller 8

The Running of a Gristmill 10

Water Power 12

Millstones 14

Oliver Evans 15

The Water Mill 20

Family Mills at Work 94

The Best Flour 112

Sawmills 116

Windmills 120

Post Mills 124

Tower Mills 134

A New Life for Mills 160

Glossary 247

Acknowledgments 253

Bibliography/Credits 254

Introduction

This is an illustrated documentary for the general reader, about rural mills, particularly those family-owned custom watermills and windmills, where the locals brought their harvested grain or lumber, or both, to be turned into flour or planks for a fee or perhaps a percentage of the wagon load. What was once a common occurrence is now rare, but a number of these stout buildings remain in what were strategic and active spots on stream banks and hillocks, some working, some with a new life as a home or office, some as picturesque ruins, and importantly, a growing number restored as plain country mills as interpretive museums—indicators of the growing interest in their history and technology with an eye perhaps toward their relevance as sustainable users of natural power.

Throughout the western world, out in the country, there is one building that has a universal style. Most rural folk and vernacular buildings identify their national characteristics by the angles of their roofs, styles of fenestration and doorways, how they group together, and different choices of wood, brick, or stone. There is one exception: the village mill looks similar in all countries. And it's not just because of the familiar water-wheel on one side, or the four sails above. The common proportions, the size of the millstones, the length of the sails are, on average, the same everywhere. Whether driven by the flow of streams, tides, or the power of wind, the exterior appearance, and most surprisingly, the interior workings are, except to the eyes of experienced millwrights, alike. There is a value in the physics and commonness that attested to the amount of work a family mill could do in a day and created universal patterns. Within that commonness, unlike some of the mail-ordered barns of the nineteenth century, no two mills are exactly alike. The shape and flow of a stream and the wind on a hill are always a little bit different from the next. That's what makes them interesting.

My interest was drawn to mills from my work in documenting the design and usefulness of historic working buildings, with an emphasis on how they were built as much as what they were used for. With mills you soon get away from concentrating on the exterior of the structure. Once inside an old mill you must duck your head and tread carefully. There are few conventional sectioned chambers and ceiling levels. You are inside a machine, mostly wooden, but a large and powerful one, which rumbles and hums as a gristmill, and whines and screeches as a sawmill.

The remaining mills, outnumbered by barns and other worthwhile country buildings, get our particular attention because their location, or "seating," at river crossings or at the top of an open hill, are frequently regarded as picturesque. The historic-looking Mabry Mill, on the deliberately scenic Blue Ridge Parkway, as it comes into view is absurdly pretty, an image for table mats, jigsaw puzzles, and greeting cards. But if you make a visit, you will find out that this was a twentieth-century building built in 1910; that Ed Mabry had been there to grind corn, saw wood, was the blacksmith, made wagon wheels, and earned the reputation, until his back gave out, of fixing everything.

There is an aesthetic paradox about mills: there's the calendar-picture version and there's William Blake's dark, satanic versions. In between are the stone-and-brick-walled mills, such as those put up by the Shakers, beautiful in a different way, spare and honest. But the real beauty of old mills is inside them. Like Shaker buildings which grew from the nature of work, one can appreciate the way that wood can be made to move smoothly, like the insides of a large clock—the meshing of cogs made of hickory, on wheels made of oak. A mill was designed to be an engine first, its definition is to "comminute," to pulverize, to turn into powder. The woodwork gets a patina from use. Just as barn posts become sleek and honey-colored from the constant abrasion of hay and animals, mill surfaces are worn and then polished by the gentle rubbing of flour. Our regard for the country mill grows as we realize each day that the speed at which we moved away from natural, sustainable power lost us some ingenuity and skills that may be useful in the future.

The familiar image of a country mill illustrates the affection with which they are regarded. Here, the aim is to tell the story of the whole mill, to respect those who keep them going, and to visit mills with new owners who have maintained and preserved these sometimes awkward structures by adapting to the mill's spirit rather than taking advantage of its location. All mill owners deserve our gratitude for keeping this part of our history and culture alive.

The Country Miller

Before the Industrial Revolution and for some time afterwards, the miller was generally regarded as a prosperous man, and often a versatile one. He could be a jolly or morose host, and in rich land with a constant flow of water and a steady income he invariably prospered ahead of others. That he remained in a place somewhat isolated got people's attention. Millers stayed where they were, everyone came to them. The mill was the center of the community and, apart from the blacksmith, was where you would find the village engineer. He knew the intricacies of the mill and carried out repairs when needed, if necessary remaking parts himself; he was a good judge of his water or wind supply, and most of all he was a good judge of the density and content of the grain, which varied with a wet or dry harvest and the skill used in threshing and winnowing, and had many opportunities for sharp practice. He would run through a sample with his finger and thumb, calculate its value, and made his wealth that way. In the old world the miller was sometimes disliked or mocked, often out of of jealousy. Those less able considered him too much of an expert.

In still earlier times the miller worked for a landowner, and tolls for the grist were set by the manor, so the miller was resented as being part of the establishment. For the settlers in the New World things were different, with fewer of the restraints imposed by the practices of European feudalism. The farmers were free to go to whatever mill they wished, but there were rules about the size of the tolls. The miller's toll was a customary part of the transaction. He kept a percentage, sometimes called a "pottle" varying between a quarter and a fifth of the grain brought to the mill. But it varied everywhere; in 1663, Virginia a sixth was officially stated, and in 1800, Vermont millers thought that a fourteenth was about right. Vermont was said to be the home of the saying, "you can never tell upon whose grain the miller's pig was fattened." And the canny housewife "measured before and after sending to the mill."

He was a master hand at stealing grain
He felt with his thumb and thus he knew
Its quality and took three times his due
—Geoffrey Chaucer
in the "Reeve's Tale" from *The Canterbury Tales*

But most millers were honest, the word of a dishonest miller would spread and he would soon lose all of his business. Hence, "never take a toll from a widow's grist, or from a man bringing his grain on his back."

The stone, or milling, floor of Eastham Windmill, Massachusetts.

The Running of a Gristmill

The machinery inside the earliest mills was as simple as the general architecture of the buildings. Wooden wheels made of oak meshed with teeth made of apple or hickory wood. The grain was ground between two large burr stones assembled from hard French granite, if the miller could get them. The capstone, which was moveable, revolved barely above the lower stone, which remained stationary. The grain was fed into the upper stone through a funnel and the crushed meal was pushed outward. As the flour fell away from the stones, it was collected for the next process, which consisted of sending it through silk screens before it finally reached the waiting sacks. There were no quick starts or stops in an old mill. In starting the mill, water was released gradually until the wheel was running at the desired speed. In stopping the mill, the miller tried to avoid backlash to the capstone as momentum slackened.

The grain poured from a hopper into the eye of the capstone. Its flow was controlled by an angled wooden shoe and by the action of the dansil, most often called the damsel, a device attached to the spindle that tapped the shoe and shook an even amount into the millstones at every revolution. The crushed grain was forced outwards toward the edge of the stones as flour, then into a scoop on the side of the bedstone.

I have heard several definitions of the expression "keeping one's nose to the grindstone," but appropriately it refers to the attentive miller paying close attention to the distance between his stones while they are running. Having the stones too close or "thin" meant that the mill would be filled with a sulphurous stink and not too far away from combustion. Millers had to listen too. Oliver Evans said that the miller should listen to the "noise of the damsel," not in distress, but for changes in its rhythm as it shook the grain into the eye of the top stone.

If the action be too great
  Then add a little feed and weight;
But if the motion be too slow
  Less feed and weight will let her go
                    Oliver Evans

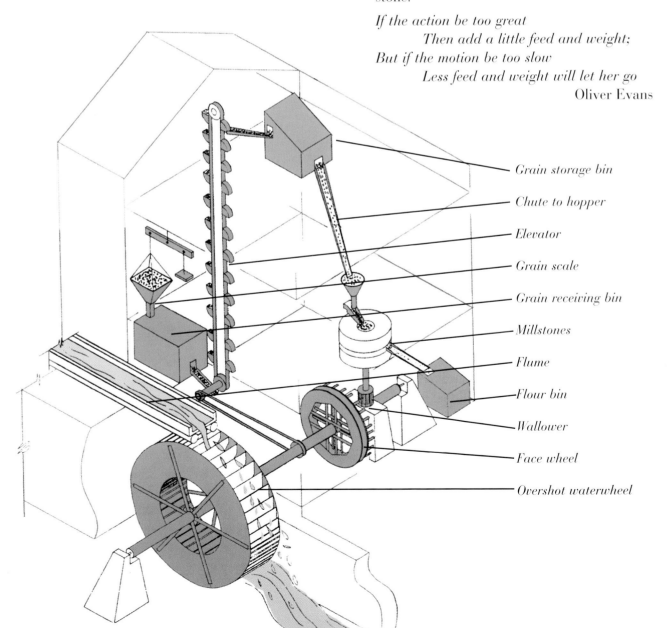

Grain storage bin

Chute to hopper

Elevator

Grain scale

Grain receiving bin

Millstones

Flume

Flour bin

Wallower

Face wheel

Overshot waterwheel

In 1852, Samuel Fitz believed that his works in Martinsburg, West Virginia, built America's first all-metal overshot water wheel. Early Fitz overshot waterwheels, built of wood, had an efficiency of seventy five percent at best. Wooden buckets could not be curved for efficiently receiving and discharging water; and wheels were frequently out of balance and jerky in rotation. Exposed wooden wheels suffered in the winter, either freezing solid or having their weight increased by ice. They had an average life of ten to thirty years, depending on how well the wheel was maintained, which was frequently. An all-iron wheel would end all of these troubles.

Although the Fitz Company began to make all types of metal wheels and eventually turbines, their main thrust was producing overshot wheels. Over the years, the red-painted Fitz overshot wheel became a familiar sight all over America. The company claimed to have installed over one thousand water-wheels in Pennsylvania alone, and over seven hundred in the state of Virginia. And in every size: Fitz built waterwheels from four to forty five feet in diameter, and from one to sixteen feet in width. They were busy well into the twentieth century; surprisingly, the biggest year of production was 1940.

In the Fitz design, water enters the buckets ten inches behind vertical center. Because of their scientifically designed curve, the water was retained in the buckets almost to the bottom vertical position at the tail race. They were found to be ninety percent efficient.

Water Power

A tiny brook is all you need—John Fitz

Over the years people were drawn to country mills by first noticing their most attractive features: their sails and waterwheels. Today, there are very few windmills in America, and by the end of the nineteenth century many watermills had lost their outside wheels in the conversion to out-of-sight tur-bines. Farther north, millers had some protection against freezing by build-ing their wheels inside. Fortunately, there are still enough watermills working or standing to explain the difference in size and shape of their waterwheels. There was no established place for the wheel at the mill. It might be against the longest wall or at one end, in a narrow chamber inside, or in a separate housing.

Water power is a gift of nature. All the waterwheel does is make use of the force that already exists in the stream. Existing waterwheels on dried-up water sources are evidence of how the mill adapted to the original stream conditions. The size of each mill's waterwheel corresponded to how the water came to the mill. A fast-running, steep and narrow stream would have a large, narrow wheel. On a wide slow-moving stream the wheel would gather more water when it was wider and smaller.

The Overshot Wheel required a dam above it so that the weight of water falling on it would make it turn. After one-third of a revolution, the water was spilled from the wheel. The water first striking the wheel gave it momentum, but the weight of the water in its buckets kept it turning. Overshot wheels could be up to sixty feet in diameter and carried five or six times the number of buckets to the radius of the wheel in feet. The slow-moving wheel needed large gears that handled huge amounts of torque. Practice and experience proved that the overshot wheel was much more efficient than the undershot and breast wheels. Gradually, wooden waterwheels and other exposed moving parts of the mill were superseded by iron, which was more weather-resistant. The buckets on the wheel could be hammered or forged into shape. The wheels were seventy to ninety percent efficient.

The Undershot Wheel worked in a running stream and could turn in shallow water. It was often built by the first settlers since it was relatively simple to set up and could do simple things. It needed the running stream to make it move at all and was only thirty-five percent efficient. They were common in the early days when a dam could be built to compensate for dry periods and release some much-needed power.

The Breast Wheel, like the undershot wheel, turned in the opposite direction to the overshot wheel and received water above its center shaft at the nearest point of the water supply, and revolved easily because it was less loaded with water. It was at its most efficient when receiving a flow from an eight- to ten-foot head of water, and was never more than sixty percent efficient.

The Flutter Wheel was used when there was a large supply of water. It was small, low, and wide—about three feet in diameter and up to eight feet wide. It got its attractive name from the sound it made. As the wheel went around, the blades cut through the entering water, making a noise like the fluttering wings of a bird. It was used almost entirely to power early sawmills. It operated well with a minimum of six to eight feet of water and could supply a saw with up to 120 strokes per minute.

The Tub Wheel could only work where the water flowed regularly throughout the year, and needed at least an eight-foot fall. The tub wheel was horizontal and was described as acted upon by percussion of water. The shaft is vertical, running the stone on top of it, and serves as a spindle. The water is shot on the upper side of the wheel in the direction of a tangent fitted with blades. It revolves in a sturdy tub, projecting far enough above the wheel to prevent the water from shooting over it, and whirls above it until it strikes the buckets. The tub wheel was also used in conjunction with a flutter wheel to run a sawmill.

Also horizontal and submerged, **The Turbine**, with its curved blades, eventually replaced the waterwheel that had been spinning against the mill wall. Small, fast-running, with a smooth action, below any ice, it was the potential model for the future power plant.

In 1824, French engineer, Jean Poncelet studied the lowly undershot, the least efficient of all waterwheels, and came up with a design that more than doubled its efficiency.

Roy S. Hubbs pointed out that older undershot waterwheels presented a flat blade for the incoming water to impact, allowing half of the velocity to pass through unchecked. These losses resulted in most of the old undershot wheels performing at less than thirty percent efficiency.

The Poncelet design, on the other hand, presented a curved blade with its lip angled tangentially to the incoming water to reduce the impact to near zero. The blades of this new wheel also receded before the incoming water at one-half of its velocity, but here the water climbed up the curved incline, cresting about fifteen degrees after entry and receded to the lip in another fifteen degrees, losing most of its forward momentum, thus transferring substantially all of its energy to the wheel.

Close observation will reveal that the Poncelet design is a large turbine. It was only two or three years after Monsieur Poncelet announced his design that another Frenchman, Benoit Fourneyron, turned the wheel on its side and dropped the water into its center, allowing the water to flow simultaneously out of all the passages between the blades Thus, Monsieur Poncelet's design inspired the first practical turbine.

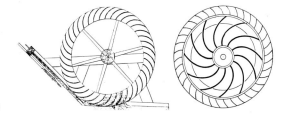

The Poncelet wheel and the turbine.

Since the turbine used all the openings between its blades simultaneously, it could be made much smaller. It turned much faster than the larger wheels. It could handle heads many times its diameter, which the larger wheels could not do. The turbine developed eighty percent efficiency, or better.

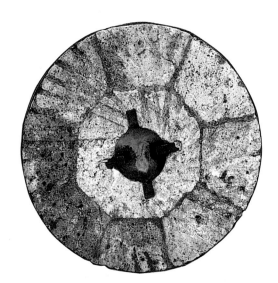

A French burr runner stone made of blocks banded with steel and backed with plaster of Paris.

A "local" runner, or upper stone, used for grinding animal feed.

An "edge runner" oil mill stone. It was used typically to crush flax seed prior to processing into linseed oil.

Millstones

Millstones had to be very hard for milling fine flour. All countries used stones out of an experience with hand grinding in querns. As they conquered Europe, the Romans recognized the quality of a dark lava stone near today's Cologne and distributed it around their empire. It also made its way to mills in colonial America. Still produced today, it is popularly known as Cullin stone. The English did their best with stone from the Pennine Hills, but for the finest flour, there was no substitute in Europe or North America for the rock unearthed in layers of clay at La Ferte-sous-Jouarre in the Marne Valley in northern France.

The French millstones were prized because their raw material, a variety of quartz, had many tiny holes in the hard flint structure of the rock. As the stone wore down, cutting edges were continuously revealed, keeping the stones hard and sharp. At the end of the eighteenth century the demand exceeded what the strand of deposits could produce as complete millstones, so production began on the now-familiar millstone made of segments from each quarry and bound together with an iron hoop, rather like fitting the tire to a cartwheel. The bands were first expanded using heat, then slipped around the stone and allowed to cool, shrinking to a very tight fit. Charles Howell, the widely respected English miller wrote that "French stones produced a whiter flour from wheat because the extremely hard nature of the stone was far less abrasive than any other stone used. An abrasive stone tends to shred the outer part of the grain of wheat—the bran—into a powder. This fine-powdered bran dresses through the fine mesh silk or woven wire of the flour dressing machinery or bolters together with the white part of the wheat meal, and the flour thus produced is of a darker color."

The furrows come out from the center of the stone tangentially, but in one direction following the eye of the stone like a Catherine wheel. The furrows are cut very carefully, not in a simple "v" but an italic "*v.*" The stones are imposed with the furrows facing each other in a mirror image. Even so, the top of the furrowed surfaces are not perfectly flat but very slightly concave. As the motion of the top stone pushes the grist out to the edge it becomes finer and finer flour. The center of stones for grinding wheat into flour were always dressed and set to be at least a sixteenth of an inch apart. The stones very gradually came closer until they were about twelve inches and converged to almost touch. From here to the rim was called "the flowing of the stone."

An old mill boasting two pairs of millstones often used the best one for flour and the other for buckwheat and cornmeal. Seldom did a miller attempt to use burrs that had been grinding cornmeal for making flour. Cornmeal has an oily exudation, which penetrates the stone and gives it a glaze that is difficult to remove. This made that stone unsatisfactory for grinding wheat.

Oliver Evans

Getting the grain to the hopper above the millstones and moving the sacks of flour was hard, backbreaking work. Oliver Evans, as a teenager, had shown his aptitude for invention and an interest in developing steam engines. In 1787, at the age of twenty-seven, he was contracted to build a mill for his two brothers. Traveling around to see other examples, he was astonished to see such an age-old and important part of daily life so badly served.

He later wrote the following description of the milling he had seen:
"If the grain be brought to the Mill by land carriage, the Miller took it on his back, a sack weighing three bushels (*180 pounds*), carried it up one story by stairsteps, emptied it in a tub (*240 pounds*)...This tub was hoisted by a jack moved by the power of the Mill, which required one man below and another above to attend to it, when up the tub was moved by hand to the granary, and emptied. All this required strong men. From the granary it was moved by hand to the hopper of the rolling screen, from the rolling screen by hand to the millstone hopper, and as ground it fell in a large trough, retaining its moisture, from thence it was with shovels put into the hoist tubs, which employed two men to attend, one below, the other above, and it was emptied in large heaps on the meal loft, and spread by shovels, and raked with rakes, to dry and cool it, but this necessary operation could not be done effectually, by all this heavy labor. It was then heaped up over the bolting hopper, which required constant attendance, day and night, and which would be frequently overfed, and passed through the cloth, which with the great quantity of dirt constantly mixing with the meal from the dirty feet of everyone who trampled in it, trailing it over the whole Mill and wasting much caused a great part of it to be condemned, for people did not even then like to eat dirt, if they could see it. After it was bolted it required much labor to mix the richest and poorest parts together, to form the standard quality; this lazy millers would always neglect, and great part would be scrapped or condemned, while others were above the standard."

Evans saw the need for an automated system and got to work, using the power of the waterwheel.

He came up with a system that could raise the grain using an elevator consisting of an endless belt fitted with wooden or metal buckets, each holding a scoopful and sending it down to the millstones below. Traditional mills then used an apprentice, called the hopper-boy, whose job was to dump the flour on the floor and rake it back and forth to reduce its heat and moisture so it would not clog the bolting screens. Then the cooled flour would have to be gathered up and carried to the bolter.

Ted Hazen in *Old Mill News* wrote,
"The elevator was an endless band with buckets or cups spaced about twelve inches apart on a belt moving over two pulleys. The top pulley was fixed to the upper floor and the lower one to the basement floor. It was all enclosed to protect the moving belt and ground grain. This elevator could elevate continuously, and thus lift three hundred bushels of grain or flour per hour. The old method was to hoist it up a tub full at a time, which was the sole work of two men."

Commenting on the importance of Evans' concepts, Eugene S. Ferguson states, "It is all but impossible for a twentieth-century mind to imagine a time when the notion of continuous production was not a self-evident proposition, yet nobody before Evans had even suggested it. Evans' new automatic system of milling made no changes in the way the grain was cleaned, ground, cooled, bolted, and packed. The changes came in the way the grain was moved from one machine to the next within the mill." With the introduction of elevators and conveyors, little labor was required beyond that necessary to start, stop, and adjust the machinery.

In the summer of 1783, Evans began working on his ideas for a mill elevator. By the end of September 1783, he had perfected the principle for his hopper-boy. The hopper-boy was a large revolving rake, adjustable on a vertical shaft by means of a cord and a balance weight. It spread the ground flour after it was ground evenly on the upper floor (called the meal loft), gradually removing its moisture so it could be properly sifted. As the rake revolved in a circle on the floor, flour was delivered from a chute at the outer circumference. Because of the angle of the sweeps on the bottom of the rake, the flour was gradually turned over and over as it moved toward the center. The hopper-boy guided it to a chute leading to the bolting hopper. Evans' new mechanical hopper-boy fit into his idea of constructing a flour mill that could manufacture flour without intensive manual labor. The problem was no one paid any serious attention to his claims.

By 1788, Oliver Evans had successfully obtained the privileges for his inventions in Delaware, Pennsylvania, and Maryland. Oliver's plan was that his brother, Joseph Evans, would tour several of the states adjacent to Delaware and interest millers in their patented milling machinery. There were no takers. Oliver Evans first charged just forty dollars per each pair of millstones in a mill for his improvements. However, there were so many infringements on his inventions that it became almost impossible to collect. Perhaps a printed description with illustrations of his "improvements to milling" would help? He started work on *The Young Mill-wright and Millers Guide*, which is still in print, the best book to be found about America's turn-of-the-eighteenth century milling, and a guide to the future of the conveyor

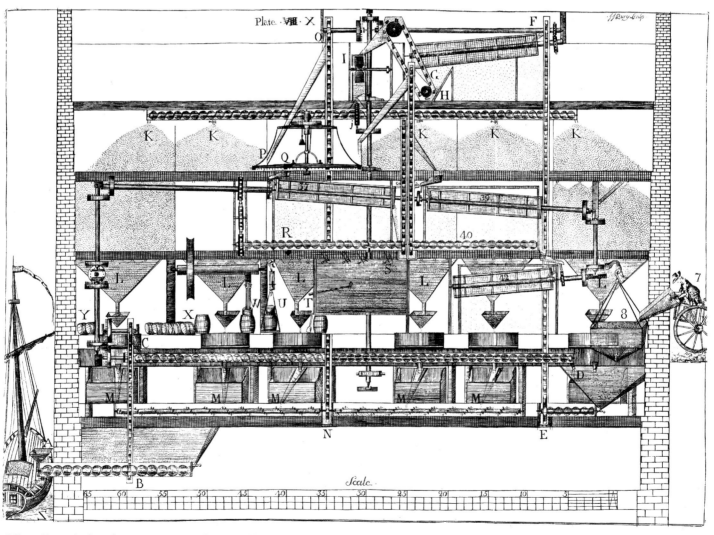

Oliver Evans' plan for an automated gristmill...

belt and automation. Although he was forced to seek private money to promote and publish his book, the word did eventually spread.

In 1791 a meeting of Liverpool, England, millers concluded:

"Mr. Oliver Evans, an ingenious American, has invented a model of a flour mill upon a curious construction, which, without the assistance of manual labor, first conveys the grain deposited to be ground to the upper floor, where it is cleaned. Thence it descends to the hopper, and after being ground in the usual way, the flour is conveyed to the upper floor, where, by a simple and ingenious contrivance, it is spread, cooled, and gradually made to pass to the bolting hopper. The whole contrivance does the greatest honor to the inventor... "

And then the English millers, like those in the United States, neglected to pay him properly for his trouble.

He knew full well the value of his inventive systems, but was a prickly character and resentful of the initial lack of respect they received, considering the nominal fees he charged. In the end, with the self-publication of his book, he practically gave his ideas away. The guide in its many editions became the standard nineteenth-century millers handbook. Throughout this volume are many examples of where Evans' work has been the criterion for the restoration of historic mills. Bringing these buildings back to work is his legacy.

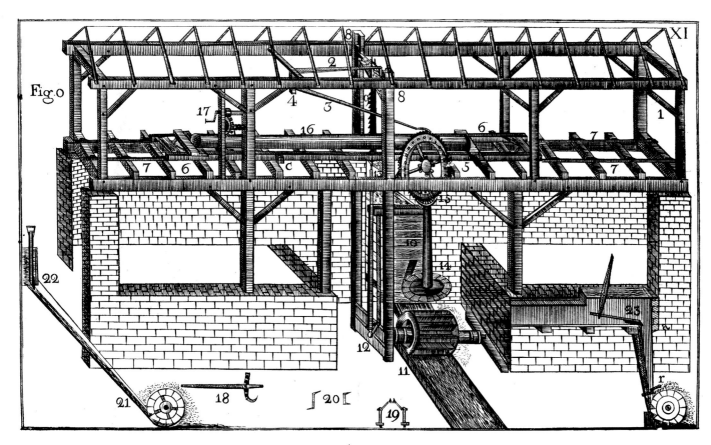

And his plan for an up-and-down sawmill. (see page 116)

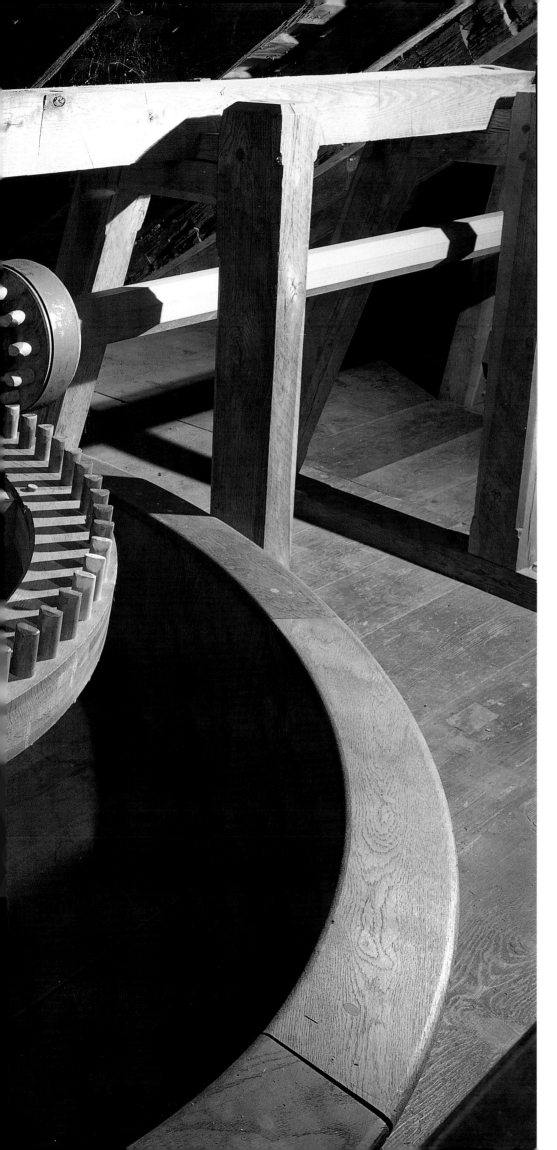

Evans' Hopper-Boy was a shallow, circular tub which contained a revolving rake. The actual size would depend on the capacity of the mill. The rake, with arms of soft poplar, was turned by a cog wheel, and it turned the flour over and over with paddles. The flour was eventually swept into a chute that directed it to the bolter below.

In operation, the rake was attached to a central, vertical shaft. A horizontal balance arm was attached to the shaft; the arm was pinned to the vertical shaft in the center. The rake itself would float upon the vertical shaft, governed by a counterweight that was tied with a rope at one end and ran up the vertical shaft through a pulley in the shaft to the rake at the opposite end. The rake had to be able to float to adjust to the volume of flour dumped into the tub. The counterweight regulated the length of the time flour spent in the hopper-boy. The rake, always on top of the flour, moved the flour in a declining spiral to an off-center discharge hole or holes. The action of the rake's paddles, or flights, turned the meal over many times before falling to the bolter.

The Water Mill

The old mills of Virginia have special value because few were built while early farmers concentrated on tobacco, and many were destroyed in the Civil War. The Colvin Run Mill, in Fairfax County, built before 1820, ground more than a million bushels for more than a century.

The handsomely restored Colvin Run Mill Historic Site was built on an ideal seating that met three criteria—location, water power, and accessibility—at the halfway point between the fertile grain-producing region of the Shenandoah Valley and the port of Alexandria. As a young building, it would have use of the latest ideas in milling technique designed by Oliver Evans and demonstrated by the Ellicott brothers in Maryland which increased the efficiency of flour production. By the mid-1930s, the family that had run the mill for 50 years had no one who wished to continue the business, so the mill was sold and went into decline. Colvin Run Mill sat by the side of the road, an eyesore, even a hazard to the community it had served for so many years. By 1965, as is so often the case, concerned citizens and the enthusiasm of members of the Society for the Preservation of Old Mills came to its rescue. In 1969 it was painstakingly reconstructed with prematurely aged materials and rescued mill workings. By 1991 the flume and the twenty-foot white oak overshot wheel with its sixty buckets were rebuilt. Today it stands as an immaculate example of a truly historic site which comes to life when visited by parties of young and old. An employee at the mill remembered the time he "watched the children's faces alight after seeing a demonstration of the beam scale with its automatic chute at the bottom. As the grain swooshed, the children giggled...The past had come alive for them."

Two of the large face wheels at Colvin Run.

The Civil War was hard on the mill. When action came to Fairfax County, the mill stood outside the perimeter of forts surrounding Washington. Unfortunately, it was not far enough outside to be beyond the reach of patrols and foraging parties from both Union and Confederate armies. As a result, milling operations became more uncertain and eventually ceased altogether. During the latter part of the war, the mill's burr stones only turned to custom grind wheat or corn for neighboring farmers who brought their grain in sacks laid across their saddles.

From Fairfax Courthouse to Petersburg, the region was such a wilderness that nature came back and deer ran through the forests. Sheridan had swept down the fertile Shenandoah Valley like an avenging fury, leaving a trail of wreckage and ruin. "We had no cattle, hogs, sheep, or horses or anything else," wrote a native of Virginia. The fences were all gone....The barns were all burned; chimneys standing without houses and houses standing without roofs, or doors, or windows....Bridges all destroyed, roads badly cut up....The entire economic life of the South was shattered.

Underneath the stone floor at Colvin Run.

In 1870, the wheat and corn crop of Virginia was about one-half of what it had been in 1860. Farms that sold for one hundred dollars an acre before the war went begging at five dollars an acre after. No banks or insurance companies were able to give credit, and farmers found they lacked the means to plant or harvest a crop, let alone get it to market. In northern Virginia of the late 1860s and early 1870s, the miller and the farmer found themselves the victims of steadily rising costs and falling prices. The mill owner struggled against bankruptcy throughout the 1870s, but by 1883, after a forced sale, the mill changed hands.

The Millard family ran the mill for fifty years and their entreprenurial spirit has been well documented. They continued to repair and restore their property— the millpond and millrace were rebuilt, the mill and its machinery were rehabilitated and progressively modernized, and the mill's century-old burr stones turned at a steady rate.

Modern technology increased the competition among millers for markets, and the Millards were quite successful. In the 1920s, their mill served not only the neighborhood for many miles around, but also supplied some twenty stores in and around Washington, D.C., and Richmond. They also shipped flour and meal by rail to Ohio, New York, Maine, Pennsylvania, and Kentucky.

In 1930, Sam and Alfred Millard were interviewed for an article in the trade journal *National Miller and American Miller*. They recalled that one pair of burr stones—probably the oldest—was reserved for grinding cornmeal. Other burr stones were used for grinding whole wheat, or "health" flour. Burr stones were used to crack wheat and rollers were used to process this cracked wheat into a finer flour. Using burr stones in combination with rollers, the Millards produced about thirty-five barrels of white flour per day. By 1930, they estimated that their stones had ground over a million bushels of grain.

Modernization notwithstanding, the Millards also offered custom milling at Colvin Run Mill in much the same manner as previous owners had for one hundred years. Customers' preference for the products of a particular mill was just as strong as was their preference for other personal services—and the Millards' custom-grinding patrons extended over a wide area. Typically, they came to the mill on horseback with a sack of grain slung across the saddle or stowed in the back of a buggy or farm wagon. They might exchange their grain for flour already ground, or they might have it ground on the spot. Some customers would accept only flour made from their own grain and ground according to their own specifications.

Bernard Bailey took over the mill from the Millards and intended to remodel it and resume production of stone-ground flour and cornmeal. Because he believed that the roller milling equipment in the mill caused vibrations that endangered the old building, and that flour milled by rollers was less nutritious than stone-ground flour, Bailey announced that he intended to remove the modern equipment installed by the Millards and return to the days when grain was milled solely on grinding stones. After World War II the wooden waterwheel—warped and rotten from disuse—was replaced by an all-steel waterwheel. But as the 1950s ended, Bailey's hopes for restoring water-powered stone grinding at Colvin Run Mill came to an end. Repairs could not be made fast enough to reverse the mill's gradual deterioration, and eventually the mill became nothing more than a decrepit store. Residents, aware of the mill's importance petitioned Fairfax County to buy it. Recognized in 1964 as a condemned building, restoration of the mill began.

Fairfax County hired John E. Campbell, of Philadelphia—considered one of the leading mill restorationists in the United States—to assess the mill's condition. Following his inspection and inventory of the equipment in the mill, the county sought suitable materials of the proper historic period to be used in the restoration of Colvin Run Mill. The Kinsley Mill, near Buckland in Prince William County, Virginia, unused for many years and in a state of disrepair, was purchased and dismantled. Its salvaged materials, including several burr stones, bellows, gears, conveyor belts, and screens, were transported to Colvin Run Mill. These, however, were valuable mainly as historic artifacts. During the restoration of the mill to its original working condition, many of the wooden pieces of equipment were newly handcrafted by designer and master cabinetmaker Lowell Hott, of Arlington, Virginia. Trees in the vicinity were marked for cutting and sawing when the restoration project needed them. In addition to the wooden gears in the basement, the waterwheel and bolting chest are examples of Hott's craftsmanship. Colvin Run Mill Historic Site opened to the public in 1972.

Right:
The Bolter at Colvin Run
(see page 113)

The rich farmland and plentiful streams has given southeastern Pennsylvania a legacy of watermills larger than any other part of the United States. Although many are no longer in use, family mills are still running in this area, and there is news of restoration and reconstruction. There is an architectural style to the stone and brick mills in southeastern Pennsylvania. Here, unlike in New England or the Southern Appalachians, most mills used the overshot wheel, which produced more power, and were mounted inside the mill structure. Inside wheels were needed because so much wheat was being produced in the state that there was a need for milling all year, and inside wheels would not freeze up in the winter. In other parts of the East Coast, milling was only a seasonal occupation. The building itself is usually rectangular and the simple lines are pleasing to the eye.

Stephen Kindig, the molinologist and consultant in the restoration of historic mills, has a mill that no longer runs but is a home for the history of milling practice. Still in place are the tools and machinery that provide the visitor with a good illustration of how a one-man mill could run efficiently. The miller's tools still hang on their nails in the parts of the mill where they were needed. Overleaf are some that once kept the millstones running evenly.

The pond at Stephen Kindig's mill. The wheel was inside, and the miller's office was the attached structure on the left.

Millstones that became smooth would not grind; they needed to be roughened periodically to grind perfectly. This was called "dressing" and was a task requiring great skill and experience.

Parts of the stone's surface could be identified by using these simple looking, but very effective tools. The wooden paint staff had its surface burnished and made true after picking up an even coating of oil from the surface of the steel proof staff. Then with a coating of red oxide powder, the paint staff would be rubbed evenly across the millstone and expose the raised areas in red. Then the dresser would get to work, and with one hand balanced against the other, the surface would be picked. Making a new, abrasive area was done with firmness rather than force, more action coming from the wrist than the arm. The blows were delivered with the full width of the sharp edge, making patterns of about twenty five-marks to the inch.

The expression "show me your metal" originated in the milling fraternity, directing a person to prove what he said he was and what he could do. A millstone dresser would pull up his sleeves revealing the mark of his trade on his hands and forearms, which were speckled blue from chips lodged under his skin. This did not mean he was highly skilled at dressing millstones, but that he had experience in dressing them. It also showed that his picks might have been tempered too hard.

proof staff

paint staff

At the end of the stick coming from the millstone spindle is a quill that checks the true level of the stone by scratching its surface.

30

An automatic bell alarm tells the miller when the hoppers are running empty. The miller nailed a piece of leather inside the hopper, and fastened a string to the other end. The string was then passed out the side of the hopper and attached to a bell. As long as the grain rests on the leather and presses it down, the string stays taut and the bell out of reach of the machinery. When the grain in the hopper runs low, the weight of grain is removed from the leather, which is pulled up by the bell at the other end of the string. The bell then hangs sufficiently lower to be struck by some part of the machinery, thus warning the miller.

This is a locally quarried feed stone at the Kindig mill. On top of the runner are stone dressing tools and picks. In the center of the stone, under the arms of the lifting bails, is a damsel. To the left of the spout (foreground) is a tentering wheel which, when turned, adjusted the clearance between the millstones by raising the upper stone.

Mill Springs Grist Mill, near Monticello, Kentucky, is on a two hundred-year-old mill site. The power for its wheel comes from thirteen springs on the steep hill-side. They combine to form one cascading stream toward the pipe that ends just above the giant, overshot forty-foot wheel.

The white clapboard mill rests on a stone foundation and overlooks Lake Cumberland. This scenic area was also a Civil War battleground where the opening battle for the Kentucky-Tennessee campaign was fought. The mill owner's house served as headquarters for the Confederate forces. The present mill structure dates from 1874.

In 1908, following the trends of the times, miller Bolan E. Roberts adapted the mill to accommodate three roller mill stands and needed more power. The solution was a bigger wheel made of steel to replace the twenty-eight-foot wooden one. The forty-foot Fitz waterwheel is the main attraction for visitors. It is the largest waterwheel still grinding in the United States. In John Fitz's design, water enters the buckets of the wheel just ten inches before its vertical center. Because of the buckets' scientifically designed curves, the water is retained almost to the bottom vertical position at the tail race. A wheel like this is almost ninety percent efficient.

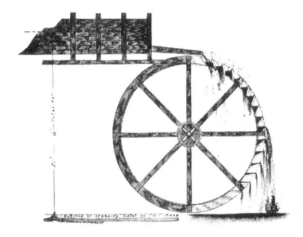

This illustration, produced by the Fitz Company, shows the inefficiency of a wooden wheel that could not have curve-shaped buckets, as shown on the one below.

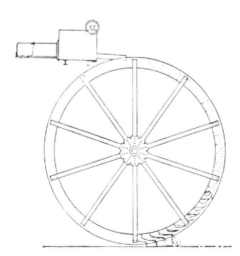

Here, the water arrives about ten inches short of the wheel's vertical center, and the curved buckets begin to fill just as they pass over the top of the wheel.

The federal government acquired the mill and the surrounding land in 1949. The state of the mill declined, being used very occasionally for tourists. Although listed on the National Register of Historic Places, the mill, which had in its working days been modified continuously to accept new machinery and was perched on steep ground, became rundown and unsafe. After complete restoration in 1976, the mill is an attractive example of a working building in its prosperous period.

Because of their often attractive settings, water mills have been used throughout history as trysting places for lovers. Today they are often chosen as spots to get married. In the middle distance, seen through the great wheel, a ceremony takes place.

The workings of the mill's main driveshaft are easily seen from a walkway under the main floor. The belts connect to the stones above, where corn is ground on weekends.

41

The controlled stretch of water from the dam had several names, usually called the sluice, but also known as the race, wooden ditch, wooden pipe, flume, or penstock. Here, at the Mingus Mill in North Carolina, a wooden trestle supports the sluice on its way to the turbine. The passage of water was controlled by a gate nearest the mill—the last body of water before the wheel—and was sometimes a wooden canal raised on a trestle leveled to approach the wheel at the most effective height. Just before the flow neared the wheel or turbine housing, a rack would be erected to keep out any debris.

The restored Mingus Mill is a fine example of the work of the young men in the Civilian Conservation Corps in the 1930s. The mill sits at the southern end of the Blue Ridge Parkway among other examples of restoration, landscaping, and civil engineering made with the labor of previously unemployed twenty-year-olds given the opportunity to do useful work, learn skills, and help America out of the Depression. More than sixty years later, the plain but honest Mingus Mill is a monument to the value of a program that has paid for its original costs several times over.

In its present state the interior of the Mingus Mill is as stark as the exterior, with light creeping in through the clapboard walls. There is a reason for this: the mill serves primarily as an excellent example for its many visitors of how meal is ground. The only working parts of the mill are the grindstones, driven by the turbine below. As in some other government places, the old-fashioned methods do not meet today's federal health standards and it cannot sell what it produces. However, the mill really comes to life when one of the roster of volunteer millers gathers a group together and describes his work and the life of a mill, while a fellow miller releases the flow and gets the stones turning.

A visit to Mabry Mill at milepost 176, on the Blue Ridge Parkway, in a picture-postcard setting, is worth more than a photo opportunity. It serves best as a well-documented example of a one-man industry between the years of 1903 and 1935. In the connected and surrounding structures, you can learn that Ed Mabry ran a gristmill, a sawmill, a blacksmith shop, and with these basic works could supply the important needs of the folks around. More than that, with a jigsaw and jointer, a tongue-and-groove lathe, and a planer, he made and repaired wagon wheels and his own furniture. He was known around the area as a man who could fix almost anything.

Spring Mill, in Mitchell, Indiana, is larger than most country mills, and is certainly one of the best built in the United States. It is an operating mill and sells its own cornmeal to visitors. Historians believe the mill was erected in just six months and was ready for work in the fall of 1817. When it was completed, the mill was a tribute to craftsmen of the day. The tasteful interior was trimmed with tulip poplar, the doors and casements were fashioned from black walnut, with a paneled entrance door under a fan-shaped transom. The original floors were of ash and said to be smooth enough for a ballroom. The three-story building and the supporting flume piers were built of local limestone, cut and dressed by hand. The waterwheel and the other large, wooden moving parts are made of oak. It is one of the most-visited and admired sites in the state and is maintained to a high standard by the Indiana Department of Natural Resources.

The water appears to arrive to the mill via an open flume from a dammed section of Hamer's Branch Creek. Actually the tidy-looking flume boards on the stone piers conceal a twenty-inch-diameter steel pipe that narrows to twelve inches for the last twenty feet before the wheel, where there's a control valve that regulates the flow and the speed of the wheel. The flow rate produces forty horsepower. As the machinery begins to turn, the miller regulates the flow for an even speed to be transferred from waterwheel to the grindstones. The iron pipe is necessary because the water supply is limited when the owner of the spring needs to use it.

When the mill was built it was an example of the latest technology rather than tried-and-true common practices, with its elevator and other labor-saving devices. It became so busy that farmers often had to wait nine to ten days in peak season for their corn or wheat to be ground. The mill entrance door that is used today was once the wagon entrance. Above it is the pulley that was used to raise the sacks off the wagons up to the second and third floors, which were used for grain storage. The limestone above the door is worn from the constant abrasion of sacks passing over it.

The power from the outside waterwheel engages the face wheel into a sequence of wallowers and cog wheels that turn the millstones, shown on the right. The mill machinery, the twenty-eight-inch thick shaft (shown above), the cogs, pinions, and other moving parts were of wood—all hand-carved with marvelous skill.

The original five-foot-wide French burr grindstones, which can be seen on display inside the mill, were shipped from France to New Orleans, then transported up the Mississippi and Ohio Rivers on a flat boat to Louisville. The one-ton stones were then pulled by teams of oxen to the mill site.

The up-and-down sawmill has a separate, smaller undershot
flutter wheel, which gets its water supply from a pipe connected
to the main flume. A tub wheel rachets the log carriage forward
for the next cut.

The French and Pickering Creeks Association Conservation Trust worked hard
for twenty years to preserve and restore a small mill in Chester County,
Pennsylvania, where Stephen Kindig had been instrumental in stressing the
mill's historic importance. The Trust had a friendly relationship with the miller,
who steadfastly refused to part with his mill, since he wished to leave this
world still owning it. After the miller died an aged 95 in 1982, the Trust
acquired the property. In their preservation efforts, they published a well-
produced and concise booklet about the history and significance of this unique
mid-eighteenth century building; unique because it carried on as a mill with its
original machinery far longer than would be expected, and it was not until
1820 that some of Oliver Evans' inventions were added. A selection of the
researchers' and contributors' comments follow.

Toward the middle of the eighteenth-century, Samuel Lightfoot built a gristmill at Anselma, on the Pickering Creek. For more than 170 years the mill became the center of a small community that included its store, a post office, a branch of the railroad, and a creamery. In 1919, Oliver E. Collins bought the mill for $2,800. Under Collins the mill began the transition from a community enterprise to the embodiment of a single man's ability to forge a twentieth-century living from eighteenth-century technology.

No less a miller than his predecessors, Oliver Collins continued to honor the miller's primary purpose of grinding grain by maintaining the age-old process and machinery. While he created new function to supplant a dying gristmill business, Collins never changed the mill itself or discarded any of its contents. Demonstrating true country ingenuity, he successfully operated a sawmill, a cider press, metalworking machinery, the Anselma Post Office, and did lawn mower repairs and barbering to support himself, his family and his beloved mill. Superseded by a faster-moving technology, his installations represent a way of industrial life as obsolete in today's world as that of his predecessors.

The mill at Anselma, and its collection of machinery, is remarkable and unique on a variety of levels.

Stephen J. Kindig, the consultant for historic mills said: "I have never found an example to equal this mill. Whereas there are several partial examples extant, the mill at Anselma is the only one complete in all the necessary machinery—of the 'Wooden Age'—to produce 'white flour' from wheat and animal feed from various other grains.

"The basic technology of this industrial artifact is that of the mid-eighteenth-century, adapted to make use of several of the automating inventions of the famous eighteenth-century American inventor Oliver Evans. Evans is credited with being the originator, through his milling inventions, of the concept of automation—the basis of most industrial processes.

"The inclusion of these inventions in countless American mills from 1790 on caused the United States to attain its still-enjoyed position of being 'miller to the world.' The Mill is of great importance because it is the prime known example of pre-Evans technology, allowing the interested observer to understand clearly the extraordinary impact that his inventions, through their addition to the existing 'state-of-the-art' machinery, had on milling technology. Here is an opportunity to preserve the most complete example of this milling system known to exist."

In his appraisal of the mill, John Tyler, a former curator at the William Penn Memorial Museum, noted that the small size of the mill is important because most mid-eighteenth century mills were torn down in the nineteenth century or rebuilt so as to be unrecognizable. A mill 25-by-45 feet is most rare. Tyler dated the 1820–30 milling machinery through close examination of nails and construction:
"To find one of the above small mills is difficult enough. To find one that retains its original-type machinery is almost impossible. The machinery that we see in place today is of the exact original type, and is not usually found in such a complete form. Many times a few earlier parts will remain in service in a mill, but hardly ever have I seen total retention of original-type gearing and shafts.

"I was particularly pleased to see several features of the early mill that I have not been able to find up to now. One was the survival of the bolting, or sifting, machine on the upper floor. This is the revolving, silk-covered drum inside the wooden box. Generally, these have been torn apart long ago. This is a very rare survival. Another is the survival of the many decorative touches in the woodwork and bins of the mill. The early-style newel posts, scalloped grain-chute ends, the latch on the office door—all are delightful and important additions to the character of the building."

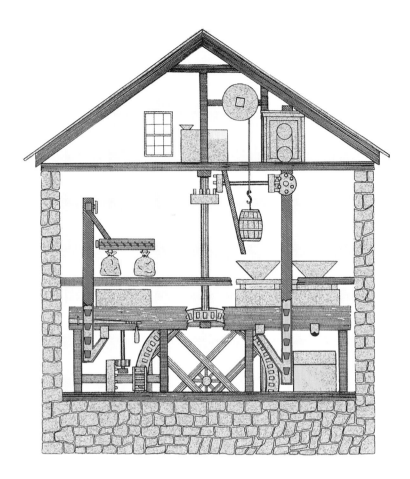

This illustration, adapted from the one prepared for the Conservation Trust, highlights in red the nineteenth century adaptations to its workings.

The mill at Anselma remains a unique example of pre-Oliver Evans technology. Conventional for that period, the mill's operation was extremely labor-intensive.

Wheat and corn were delivered and lifted by a water-powered rope hoist to the upper floor, and into a grain-cleaning machine to remove dirt and chaff. The wheat then dropped through a chute to the millstones, where it was ground. The ground wheat, now meal, dropped to a bin on the basement level. Hoisted back to the upper floor, it was then fed into the bolting reel and sifted through revolving silk screens which separated the flour from the bran and middlings. The flour was finally scooped into barrels and packed for shipping.

In 1795 Oliver Evans, a native of Wilmington, Delaware, published *The Young Mill-wright and Miller's Guide*, describing his revolutionary ideas for the "automatic" flour mill. Judging from the machinery still in place, this technology was introduced at the mill at Anselma.

Here at the mill, we clearly see eighteenth-century processes overlaid with nineteenth-century industrialization, as the miller strove to keep pace with commercial innovations.

When Oliver Collins purchased the mill at Anselma, the milling of wheat had all but ceased and the need for a gristmill would soon disappear. Undaunted, Collins overhauled the millworks and, with horses and scoop, cleaned the millraces. Faced with a changing rural economy, Collins relied on the hydraulic power provided by an eighteenth century mill to adapt to the demands of the twentieth century. The wooden master wheel, twelve feet in diameter, moved at about eight revolutions per minute. It was lubricated with melted tallow. "That had to be done about once a month," said Collins. "We had to put in new teeth every year." The huge wheel's teeth are carved from hickory, while the rim is made of oak. Smaller wheels that moved faster required twice-a-year teeth changes.

The story of the mill at Anselma involves more than this extraordinary collection within the mill itself. At its busiest period in the nineteenth century, the Anselma district included a springhouse, two homes, two barns, post office, creamery/ice house, railroad station and general store/warehouse operation. The importance of the mill to this area's growth is reflected in these additional structures that it fostered, as well as in the countless press clippings, advertisements, and correspondence that emanated from this one site.

At the Old Mill

Radiant day is slowly fading,
And the evening calm and still,
Grazing through the oak and willow,
Stoops to kiss the ancient mill.
Listen to the damsel dancing,
To the jig of feed and flour,
And the waterwheel revolving
With a dashing constant power.
There is music in the rattle
Of the tinkling wheat that falls
In the hopper, as the miller
Stops to heed the gristman's calls.
Yes, I love this shaded building,
Love the flowing stream and flowers,
Love to hear the busy clatter
On the lingering summer hours.
More than all, I love the miller,
For his sake, I love the rest.
Of this world and its enchantments
I adore him as the best.
Of these twilights I would weary
If his voice came not to cheer,
And this mill life would grow dreary
If my darling were not here.

> *Sarah Louis Vickers Oberholtzer,*
> *wife of the miller.*
> *Written at the Mill at Anselma in 1873*

In 1972, Floyd Harwood, the widely respected senior member of the Society for the Preservation of Old Mills, bought the property next to his farmstead in East Hartford, New York. He and his wife, Mildred, became the owners of a gristmill, its millhouse, and a barn. They decided to restore the buildings and create a working history museum. There was a lot to do. The wheelpit had been used as a landfill, the old dam had breached, and the millpond had silted up. In 1977, with a new waterwheel and a new dam, the mill came to life.

The mill was built by Hezekiah Mann in 1810 and operated from 1874 to 1902 by Sidney B. Weer. Today, the mill is powered by a breast waterwheel seventeen feet in diameter and six and a half feet wide. The three millstones grind flour and livestock feed. The flour is sifted by an eighteen-foot bolter. The second floor contains the transmission room and a pattern shop. An interesting lathe is driven by a nineteen-foot-long shaft. Much of the mill equipment is original.

A visit to the Log Village Gristmill Museum reveals much more than a working mill. Floyd and Mildred were teachers, and the site has expanded to be an exposition of rural life and industry, carefully labeled and arranged.

The barn houses an exhibit of old farm machinery and household items. There are many exhibits, such as walking plows, cultivators, planters, haymaking machinery, a dog-powered churn, ice-harvesting tools, corn shellers, a 150-year-old treadle wood lathe, a collection of three hundred wood planes, old boring tools, draw knives, hammers, wrenches, a hydraulic ram, water motors, a 1912 International tractor, a thresher and many old and unique items: old clothes, nineteenth century household furniture, and utensils. There are more buildings too: a cider mill, a machine shed full of buggies, wagons, and sleighs, and rising from the Harwood's dedication to teaching, is a library where one can arrange to study the collection of historic almanacs, journals, and books. As an aside, and a reflection on the respected role of the miller in a village, Floyd's neighbors will tell you that a nearby school has been named after him.

George Washington's gristmill from the west.

The tailrace.

The mill race.

The two thousand acres George Washington inherited from his half-brother Lawrence, included an old mill built in the 1730s by his father, Augustine. This mill was in a dilapidated state by the 1760s. Washington noted in his diary that it took fifty-five minutes to grind one bushel of corn. In 1769, he resolved to build a new mill, located on the opposite side of Dogue Run and about a half-mile distant from his father's. From February 1770, when Washington selected the site, with the help of John Ballendine, owner of the Occoquan Mills, a year was spent building the new mill and digging the millrace. Although some slave labor was employed in these tasks, many of the ditchers, the millwright, and the stonemasons were hired white laborers and craftsmen. This is in contrast to twenty-five years later, when one miller was hired and assisted by as many as nine slaves at the mill complex.

Typical of Washington's penchant for experimentation, he was aware of Oliver Evans' new ideas in mill technology, and in the fall of 1791, as Washington's ledger attests, Evans' brother superintended the installation of the machinery. Washington was always interested in his mill. When at home he made nearly daily visits to it, and the last journey of his life was a ride to the mill, from which he came back with a chill and was soon to be taken ill.

The mill continued to run for may years after Washington's death. It gradually fell to ruins but was still in existence not long before the Civil War. During the 1930s, older residents remembered it standing. The stone was taken away for other buildings until finally nothing remained but the foundation.

In the 1930s the mill was reconstructed based on current historical information, but by the end of the twentieth century, new studies and findings have revealed that a more accurate example of Washington's mill and its surroundings were needed. Within the mill itself Derek Ogden, the millwright, reported that along with components that had deteriorated, elements of the original 1930s construction needed to be replaced where a significant quantity of wooden members used in the framing and flooring were cut or finished using tools inappropriate to eighteenth-century woodworking.

Today, the re-reconstruction is nearly complete. Because of George Washington's connection to the site and his well-documented interest in and concerns about the mill, the aim is to present "the most accurate example" of an eighteenth-century gristmill "anywhere in the land."

Right
During the 1930s, reconstruction part of the old waterwheel was uncovered in the raceway. A template was made from the arc of the segment, and mathematical reconstruction of the circle found that the original wheel was sixteen feet in diameter. From the position of this section, and because the buckets were lying so that the water from the forebay would pass under and not over the wheel, it was believed that the wheel must have been of the pitch-back or breast wheel type. This photograph was taken in 1989, before the present work at the site.

Two views of the latest improvements at George Washington's gristmill. The work is to be carried out by Mount Vernon craftsmen, using tools appropriate for late-eighteenth-century woodworking.

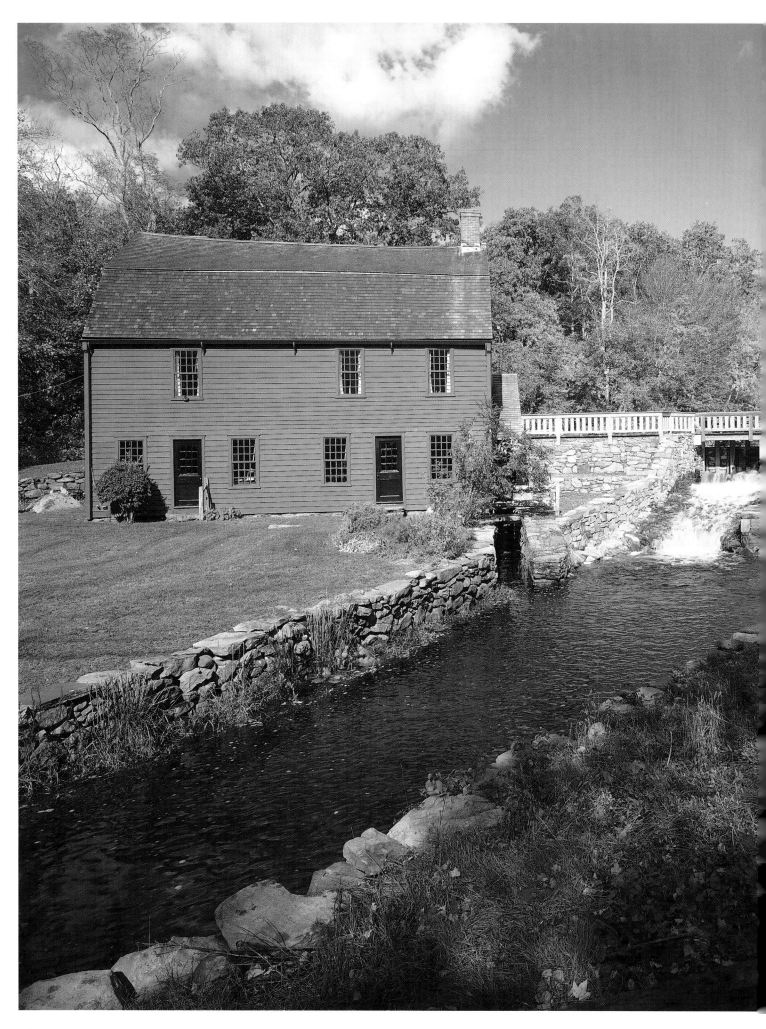

Gilbert Stuart, famous for his portrait of George Washington, was born in this snuff mill in Saunderstown, Rhode Island, in 1775. The building, with its gambrel roof, was erected in 1751, designed as a home and workplace for a miller, by Dr. William Moffat, of Newport, who wanted to compete with the snuff imported from England.

Gilbert Stewart, Sr. was hired as the miller, and lived there with his wife and children until 1761. In 1927, the Gilbert Stuart Memorial Association was formed to buy the mill from private hands and keep it in the painter's memory.

The original snuff grinding was missing, but a snuff mill of the same age was discovered in Scotland, and the association arranged to have it transported and installed at Saunderstown. The small mill, an edge-runner mortar and pestle machine, is below stairs with the other workroom of the house, the kitchen. The mill is driven by an undershot wheel and is housed under an attractive weather-protecting roof at the gable end of the house.

On the opposite bank of the Mettatuxet River is a very early gristmill, in good repair, but awaiting complete restoration.

Murray's Mill

On Ball's Creek in Eastern Catawba County, North Carolina, Murray's Mill welcomes visitors to experience the workings of a stone-ground-and-roller-flour mill. A mill was on this site as early as 1873. A decade later, William Murray purchased half the mill. In time, he and his sons, O.D. and John, would own the entire operation. By the early 1900s, they had turned the site into an industrial complex: the mill, a three-story granary, dry goods store, blacksmith shop, and lumber business. Extensive changes were made at the mill site in 1912. A new, three-story mill was built and a twenty-four-foot concrete dam was erected.

The most prosperous years of the mill followed a 1916 expansion, which added a fourth floor to the building. In 1940, the dam was raised and a larger waterwheel was installed to provide more horsepower. The mill could then produce over five hundred pounds of flour and two hundred pounds of corn meal per hour.

In 1967, the mill closed, but the Catawba County Historical Association later purchased the property and reopened the mill as an operating museum. The miller's house and the nearby store are part of the museum.

Here is a view of the underneath of the bed stones, seen through the hurst frame that supports the grinding operation. Master millwright Derek Ogden restored the massive post-and-beam timber frame.

Reduction roller stands reflect the new milling techniques available during the nineteenth century to produce "patent" flour. Two-fifths of the production milling machinery was installed at Murray's Mill between 1912 and 1913. The system was further enlarged in 1938–39, when the twenty-eight-foot Fitz waterwheel was installed with the related machinery.

Fine-crafted cabinets house the flour-sifting machinery on the second floor.
A heavy counterweight mounted below the cabinet provides the sifting action.

The Cross Mill is located along Cross Mill Road in the vicinity of the village of Cross Roads, East Hopewell Township, York County, Pennsylvania. Water power to the mill is taken from Rambo Run. Custom mills such as Cross Mill operated twenty-four hours a day, seven days a week, for months at a time. Farmers lined the road waiting their turn when their harvest was complete. While the stones ground the grain the farmers assembled in the mill office and passed the time with the miller. The Wallace-Cross family was highly esteemed in the community as good neighbors and honorable business people. The mill is believed to have been constructed in 1826, and was operated continuously until the 1980s.

The mill was placed on the Pennsylvania Inventory of Historic Places in February of 1977, and on the National Register of Historic Places in June of 1977. In 1979, the owner, a man of modest means, gave the mill, his most valuable and cherished possession, to the people of his county. Eleanor Boggs Shoemaker used to have her wheat ground at the mill. As he neared retirement, Mr. Cross told her that he would like the mill to remain standing after his death, and with her help he arranged this extraordinary gift to York County. The mill stands as a testament to their friendship and his sense of history and his abiding love of his surroundings.

At his passing the mill needed to be preserved and maintained. With the encouragement of Mrs. Shoemaker, Cross Mill has been restored through the generosity of friends and neighbors, the York County Commissioners, state and federal grants, and the York County Parks Department. A small volunteer committee has dedicated time, materials, and labor to this project. The mill will operate into the twenty-first century with the continued support of its friends and visitors.

Two views of the Cross Mill:
top, from the miller's house; right, looking up at the house.

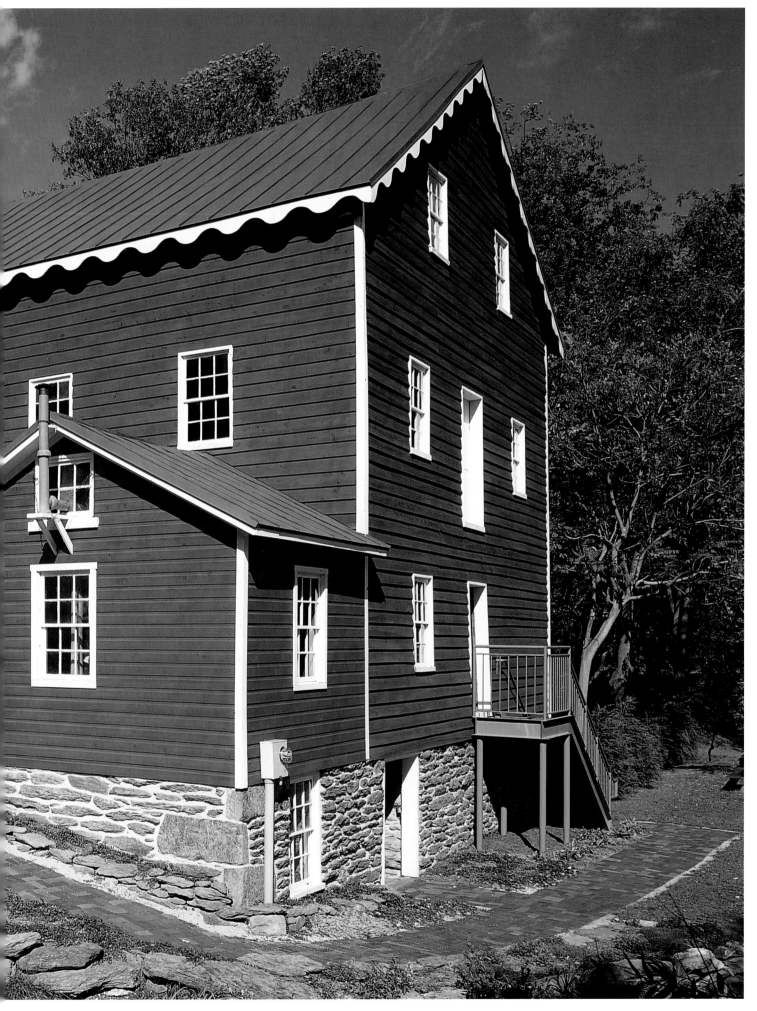

Cross Mill is a rare example of a small, rural water-powered grain mill. Most have long since been destroyed or put to uses foreign to their intended purpose. During the early part of the nineteenth century most were converted to modern roller-mill systems and had their stones removed. Turbines, followed by steam, gasoline, diesel, and finally electricity usually replaced the overshot waterwheel. The Cross Mill, tucked away in its unspoiled little valley, was bypassed by such modernization, and its basic machinery survives to demonstrate the elements basic to a rural mill.

The millstones are French buhrs, known for their superior milling qualities. The capstone is just over three feet in diameter; the bed stone is 6 inches bigger. Millstones are usually of the same diameter. In this case, the larger bed stone has been reduced in diameter to match the smaller runner—an appealing idiosyncrasy of this mill and its miller.

Next to the millstones is the stone crane, which contains a wooden screw. There are three pairs of wrought iron "bails" against the east wall. The bails, screw, and crane are used to lift the runner stone and turn it on its back for dressing. Wooden crane screws are quite rare; however, some millers preferred them to those constructed of metal.

The mill building is well designed and constructed for its specific use. The frame is entirely of oak, handhewn and properly mortised, tennoned, and pegged together. The secondary, smaller timbers such as upper floor joists show indications of having been cut on a sash ("up-and-down") sawmill. There are typical "Dutch"—divided mill doors on the first and second floors, north and south facades. The first-floor Dutch door has a latchstring, which is a cord fastened to the bar of the latch and passed through a hole in the door so the latch can be raised from the outside or pulled inside to prevent entry. A person who was known to leave the latch-string out was regarded as very hospitable. The latchstring at Cross Mill was undoubtedly always out. There is a hood roof on the north facade as an extension of the roof ridge, in which is the wood pulley for the bag hoist rope.

A British surgeon, Edward Turner Bale, shipwrecked off the California coast, built the mill in the 1840s, as the fertile Napa Valley was becoming famous as bread-basket rather than a vineyard. By 1850, the thirty-six foot wheel, made of local redwood, was busy grinding wheat, barley, and oats until a turbine took over in 1879. After 1905, the wheel, the mill house, and the 400-foot-long flume on its high trestle became over-grown with ivy. In 1923, the widow of the mill owner gave the mill to the Native Sons of the Golden West, hoping that the organization would help in its preservation and eventual restoration. It was cared for until 1941, when Napa County took over and began some restoration work. The mill's historic importance was recognized in 1974, when it became a State Historic Park. The state completed restoration of the Bale Grist Mill in 1979, and by 1989 the wheel began to turn again at its regular three-and-a-half revolutions per minute. The mill is a living-history museum rather than a fully functioning mill. As so often happens, the original flow of water is no longer what it was. Today, for demonstration purposes, recycled water is pumped up to a reconstructed section of the flume, impressive in its height, but a fraction of the original length.

Barker's Creek Mill, Dillard, Georgia, is a single-story, wood-sided mill with a rock foundation. The original wooden waterwheel was replaced in the 1960s with a locally made steel wheel measuring approximately twelve-feet in diameter. A wooden race carries water about fifty feet from the rock dam to the mill, where corn is ground by a sixteen-inch Meadows mill. This is a newer mill, with a construction date of 1944.

Falls Mill in Franklin County, Tennessee, is a fine example of a working building that became a mill. Falls Mill originated as a textile factory in the 1840s. The two owners employed twelve or so young women, as was the custom, who operated wool and cotton carding machines and a 240-spindle jack. After the Civil War, construction began on the building we see today. The stone dam was built first, holding the reserve of power to run a temporary sawmill that produced the timbers for the new factory, and the bricks were molded on the site. In 1873, the factory was completed. In 1886, the 32-foot wheel was installed to power the building as a cotton gin. In the 1920s, the waterwheel powered a generator that supplied electricity to the local community, but by 1932 the water power was insufficient to satisfy the demands of the ginning machinery. Steam, then gasoline, ran the operation.

At the end of World War II, the textile machinery was scrapped, and Falls Mill became a woodworking business that continued sporadically until 1968, but the waterwheel was still operational. Then the mill was sold to a retired couple who restored it as a gristmill with the installation of equipment acquired from a mill in nearby Winchester.

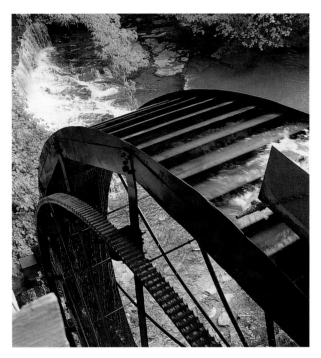

The 32-foot waterwheel is the largest in Tennessee. The owners are attentive to upkeep of the mill, with improvements to the headrace and employing a local foundry to forge a new set of 600-pound master ring-gear segments.

In the early 1980s, John and Jane Lovett, an academic couple with an interest in the history of early technology, had their dream of a living-history Museum of Power and Industry realized when they heard Falls Mill was for sale and managed to become the new owners. The mill's varied history as a rural, working building at the beginning, during, and after the Industrial Revolution has made it an ideal home for their commitment to provide an active and valuable educational resource for young and old. Visitors experience the working gristmill, the exhibits that have been gathered to tell the factory and cotton gin's history, visit the country store and buy the mill's grits, cornmeal, and flour. You can stay there, too. Falls Mill has a charming and comfortable log cabin for bed-and-breakfast accommodation.

The dramatically situated 1873 brick building is best seen from the opposite bank of Factory Creek.

Drivers who pull over to this beauty spot on the Buggaboo Creek, north of Ronda, North Carolina, will occasionally see Ralph Tharpe carefully maintaining the rock walls, grassy slopes down to the stream, and footpaths around this silent mill. It is unlikely that Tharpe's Mill will return to full operation.

Ralph's father and a partner opened the mill in 1914 and for many years the mill made a good living for the family, but in recent years the mill was no longer profitable and activity slowed down. "We opened it up again in 1981 for water ground-milling and stayed open for about a year and a half." Since then Ralph's attention has been directed toward looking after the building and the grounds.

The original dam was downstream of the present dam, and was destroyed by a flood in 1940. The Tharps built a new dam to supply the new overshot wheel that was assembled at the site and installed in 1941. Tharpe's Mill was a commercial mill for cornmeal and animal feed, but did some custom grinding. Before installation of the overshot wheel the mill was subject to the whims of the creek. "When the water was low, there wasn't enough flow to turn the wheel," Tharpe recalls. Today, Buggaboo Creek flows by the still wheel, but given the growing interest in preserving great old mills like this one, it is unlikely that Tharpe's Mill will disappear.

Lange's Mill, near Doss, Texas, is another example of a mill that formed a community. The mill itself was established in 1849, by the Doss brothers, but it was later renamed for William F. Lange, who ran the mill from 1859 to 1878. In 1880 the community that grew up around Lange's Mill received its mail from Cherry Spring. A post office called Lange was established at the community in 1898, with Julius Lange as postmaster. In 1914 the Lange's Mill community comprised some 150 residents, a Baptist and a Lutheran church, and a general store. No longer working, the sturdy mill is still owned by the Lange family, though it has been closed to prevent vandalism.

The Bagley Tunnel Mill, at Animas Ghost Town in Colorado's San Juan Mountains, was built in the hopes that the owner would find large amounts of high-paying ore and that the mill would get its own spur of a planned railroad. Some grading was done, but at over 11,000 feet, the original plans were never viable. The high snowfalls are gradually collapsing the structure. It was once said by a local magistrate that because the town of Animas Forks was at such a high elevation, there was no appeal to a verdict rendered there, it was the highest court in the land.

In 1933 a developer in Little Rock, Arkansas, put up this stone-and-concrete replica of an old-fashioned and deserted mill. Apart from the stone walls and steps, everything else is made from or covered in concrete, even the waterwheel. There are no doors or glass in the windows, but real water does run over the waterwheel. Because of its indestructible qualities and its age, it qualifies to be on the National Register of Historic Places. In 1939, it looked realistic enough to make a brief appearance in the opening scenes of the film, *Gone With The Wind*.

Family Mills at Work

The interrupted roofline and additional sections at Rohrer's Mill illustrate how the building has adapted to changes in the milling business over the years. But for a mill still being run by the same family after four generations, it has changed very slowly. It was part of the early settlement of Lancaster County, Pennsylvania, and today's building replaced a very early timber-frame structure. Henry Rohrer purchased the frame mill from the Denlinger family in 1834. Following in his father's footsteps, Christian Rohrer began operating the mill in 1852, when white flour was popular. It was not until 1910 that the mill produced whole-wheat flour. Today the mill produces whole-wheat flour, corn meal, rye flour, and meal for scrapple, Pennsylvania's unique breakfast food.

The millpond and the open-sided sawmill beyond had a combined usefulness. The pond provided swimming and skating opportunities and was a source of ice for neighbors. The ice, cut in blocks, was stored in two ice houses, which were insulated with saw-dust from the sawmill, making the ice last until July or August.

These scenes illustrate that much of the Rohrer's Mill operation has remained intact for a century and a half. The water power generated from Calamus Run moves the grain elevators up and down three stories of the mill, hoists bags of grain and flour, and crushes grain between the two sets of four foot French buhrs. Things have slowed a bit since the 1930s, when business was at its peak, with 13,000 bushels of wheat ground into whole-wheat pastry flour and cracked wheat. The Landis family grows the wheat, corn, and rye on the farm that is processed in the mill. Landis bags flour for sale to local stores and co-ops. He also sells white pastry flour, bread flour, rolled and quick oats, and wheat bran, which is obtained from another local mill.

The white stone tower (above) helped to transfer power from the overshot waterwheel to the barn. At the tower, beveled gears turned the cables ninety degrees toward the barn, where machinery would thresh wheat, shred corn, fodder, and hoist hay. In the picture opposite, the contraption on the right of the millstone hoop is a governer for adjusting the height of the runner stone.

Two views of the unchanging patterns of work at Rohrer's Mill. The mill was chosen as a perfect example of an old-fashioned, farm-based family mill to visit by members attending the Society for the Preservation of Old Mills Year 2000 Conference in Pennsylvania.

The Rohrer Mill waterwheel in motion. The original, enclosed, sixteen foot waterwheel was wooden. When steel became available, it was changed to a metal wheel. The source of its water are springs that feed into the Calamus Run, a tributary of Little Beaver Creek. Gears were added later to disengage the driving wheel and allow the transference of the power source from the waterwheel to a fifteen-horsepower diesel engine in the event of a drought or if the waterwheel becomes frozen in winter. Recently, repairs on this wheel were carried out by a local Amish craftsman.

At weekends, lovers of good food enjoy their two-hour drive north from Atlanta, and arrive in the hills around Sautee, Georgia, the home of the Nora Mill Granary, and stock up on a wide variety of stone-ground products all made at the mill.

Nora Mill Granary was built in 1876 on the banks of the Chattahoochee River, in the northeast Georgia mountains. The mill itself is a large, four-story, one-hundred-foot wooden raceway powered by a turbine. On the same site there is evidence that a mill has stood for almost two hundred years, but the mill that stands today was built by a Scotsman named John Martin. Martin came to Georgia to mine for gold, but unlike most miners, made Nacoochee Valley his permanent home.

In 1905, Lamartine Hardman, a former Governor of Georgia, bought the mill and named it Nora Mill in memory of his sister. Nora Mill remained in the Hardman family until 1998 when it, along with three hundred surrounding acres, was purchased by Tom Slick with Nacoochee Village, Ltd. After a succession of millers, the Fain family are in charge.

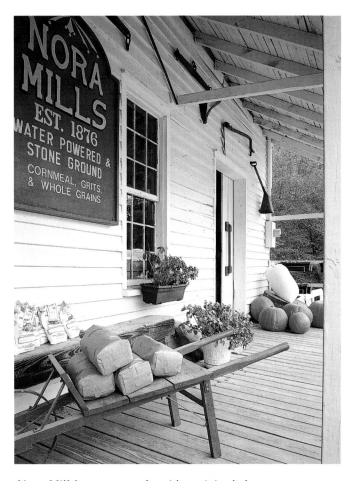

Nora Mill has two porches (the original shown here) and a new one that overlooks the mill's own gigantic rainbow trout swimming in the Chattahoochee River.

A look into the first floor of the mill from the attached country store.

The Fain Family roots began in the northeast Georgia area, just a few miles from Nora Mill. Grandpa George Fain, until his passing in 1992, ran the mill with his son, Ron, who moved into the area after retiring from the U.S. Army as a lieutenant colonel in 1979. Ron and Rita, with their five children, returned to the old family home in nearby Helen. As Ron got involved with Nora Mill, he became so interested in preserving a bit of history that he buried himself in books and publications and sought help from knowledgeable individuals including the longtime miller of Nora Mill, Tom Farmer, and Clyde Keltner, of Tennessee. Now educated in the lost art of grain milling by water power, Ron stays active in the Society for the Preservation of Old Mills.

Today at Nora Mill, the original, 1,500-pound stones that labored in 1876 still turn and grind the grains sold there. There have been many changes over the years, but the main idea is still the same: to grind fresh grains with no additives or preservatives and with old-fashioned quality. Nora Mill has recently gone through a major refurbishing. The raceway and penstock have been rebuilt, and the dam is being replaced.

The mill uses corn and wheat grown by a local farmer, and produces its nationally famous grits; white or yellow cornmeal; whole wheat, buckwheat, and rye flour; and several pancake and muffin mixes. There are no preservatives in the whole-grain products, so customers are informed to store what they buy in a refrigerator or freezer. In a corner, one can try a free sample of the mill's unique Pioneer Porridge, peruse recipes, or buy the mill's cookbook, written by Ron's daughter Janet. The mill now has an extensive mail order business and a well-designed Internet site.

Visitors are surrounded by the mill's conveyor shafts, wooden cogs, and lantern gears, along with the more familiar millstones, all carefully and descriptively labeled. There is always a member of the Fain family to tell more. Joann Vandegriff, Ron's daughter, told a visitor, "When the stone is turning, it develops a rhythm all its own. I remember looking over and seeing Grandpa Fain clapping his hands softly together and tapping his foot to the rhythm."

Kenyon Corn Meal Company is a turn-of-the-century gristmill dating back to the early 1700s, and through its history holds a reputation for quality. This view through the doorway of the new 1886 building shows that little has changed since its construction. Being ground is the mill's famous johnnycake meal. In the background is the mill's massive stone crane.

The original johnnycakes, made by early settlers, were a mixture of water and corn meal spread thin and cooked over an open fire. Johnnycakes have been maintained through the centuries and their history and controversy have become legendary. The mill's recipe dates from the time when the mill was rebuilt, but all Rhode Islanders agree that there is only one correct recipe—and that is their own.

Paul Drumm, Jr., and his son, Paul III, have owned the mill since 1971, and only use millstones for their wide variety of wholesome meals and flours, and their mixes made from them. The mill is devoted to offering ingredients that a health-conscious society looks for today, ground the simple, old-fashioned way, with no additives or preservatives. Their staunch adherence to the old techniques does not keep them from using the up-and-coming exciting new grains, including spelt, Kamut®, and blue corn, many of which are organically grown.

Wade's Mill, listed on the National Register of Historic Places, is a working flour mill, built around 1750 by Captain Joseph Kennedy. Captain Kennedy was a Scotch-Irishman who was one of the earlier settlers in the Shenandoah Valley of Virginia, between Staunton and Lexington, Virginia. This was the frontier of the United States between 1740 and 1770. The Kennedy family owned the mill for about a hundred years. The original structure burned down in 1873, but was rebuilt in the same year using the three limestone walls left standing after the fire.

In 1882, James F. Wade bought the mill and his family operated it for the next four generations. The interior and workings of the mill are much like they were when Mr. Wade took over. The mill is powered by a 21-foot waterwheel that is fed by a nearby stream (known originally as Captain Joseph Kennedy's Mill Creek).

The steel flume pipe turns into a "gooseneck"
as it rises above the overshot wheel.

As a typical southern mill, its product ranged from refined white flour to animal feed. As a small commercial mill it had difficult times from the 1960s, when large supermarkets forced the surrounding country stores out of business. The grain farms were converting to livestock, and more women had jobs and less time at home for baking. By the 1990s the growing public awareness for pure food and stone-ground cereals gave a new lease on life to the mill, and it was acquired by Jim and Georgie Young, who were determined to work hard with new ideas to keep a traditional mill going. Charlie Wade, the original miller, lives nearby and keeps up his family's long association with Wade's Mill. He is there for advice and occasionally dresses the stones. Members of his young family also help at the mill.

At the end of a road nestling in the Shenandoah Valley, the mill is an attractive place to visit. The new owners sell a wide range of flour and mixes produced by the millstones and a have made the mill a center for all things connected to good food: gifts; quality bakeware, kitchen utensils and tools; cooking classes by local chefs; luncheons; lectures; and group visits to sample the cooking of other regions and countries. In all, Wade's Mill is an example of how the mill can return as the center of a rural community. It deserves to succeed.

Jim Young, the owner, and Charlie Wade carefully raise a runner stone.

A southern mill is out of business when the water wheel is frozen.

Wade's Mill is proud of its unusual barrel packer.

Above: A miller's view of the Shenandoah Valley.

The Youngs restored the mill to its original appearance by replacing all the exterior timbers and reappointing the stone masonry.

The bolter at Murray's Mill. Originally, silk cloths topped the sifting screens. Between batches of flour production these silk screens were stored in a cedar cabinet to prevent moth infestation.

The Best Flour

The small gristmills producing pure stone ground meal make sure their customers know that fresh, unpreserved flour when not used (as best) immediately needs to be kept cool, or refrigerated. Even then, it's best to follow the miller's words on its life expectancy. Getting the meal just right and having a reputation for consistency is the real art of the miller.

Oliver Evans said that millers could see how good their meal was by trying the following: "Catch the hand full and hold the palm up, shut it briskly if a great quantity of meal flies out and escapes between your fingers. It shows it to be in a fine and lively state. But if the meal feels smooth and oily and sticks too much to the hand, it shows to be too low ground, hard-pressed and the stones dull."

The first step in producing good flour from a country mill is to know that the wheat grains were cleanly threshed and did not come from a combine harvester mixed in with bits of straw and unknown material. Most millers agree that "the finer the flour, the whiter the color." With the brown skin of the wheatberries first flaking off under the runner stone as bran, the meal has a fine mixture of particles, resulting in whole-meal flour.

Most of the inventions in milling have been machines that improve what happens to the meal after it is ground, and they increasingly took up more space in the crowded mill. The demand for white flour was the greatest so the miller put the meal through a bolter or dresser, which was connected to the same power source by a belt and pulley.

The meal was fed into the bolter, a revolving cylinder sloping downward, often in an enclosed cabinet. As it spun, the finest meal was sifted through closely meshed silk into a chute. The remainder made its way through increasingly coarser meshes and other chutes, coming out as whole-meal flour, middlings, or just bran. A good miller could divide the grain into various textures as custom demanded, or regrind the coarse meal into another mixture—Cream of Wheat originated this way.

But the argument among traditional millers was, and is, whether stone-ground or roller-machine flour was superior. In many cases, millers use both grinding methods, but those advertising stone-ground meal usually attract the most customers.

Here is in excerpt from Ed Behr's *The Art of Eating:*
In *English Bread and Yeast Cookery*, Elizabeth David mentions a flour from Holme Mills, in Bedfordshire, where the rollers are said to turn at a third of the usual rate. (They are driven, eccentrically, by an old water-wheel.) She says the flour is "attractively creamy, flecked with the smallest of straw-yellow particles" from the germ. Her demanding palate places it on a par with stone-ground. And she believes that "the real taste of the wheat is in the germ." I suspect the bran and germ in this flour are removed and the germ is then added back, a technical possibility in a roller mill. Karen Hess, who prepared notes for the American edition of the book and who has a sharp critical sense, adds that the bread baked from this flour has "a fragrance and taste of lovely wheat."

The word "bolter" has an interesting collection of origins. It is said that in 1502 Nicholas Boller, or Bolter, an Austrian, invented his sifting machine, but its origin may be older, or French. The English surname Boulter is of occupational origin, belonging to that group of surnames derived from the trade or profession of the original bearer. In this case the surname traces its root to the Old French term "buletior," meaning a "sifter of meal"; the original bearer would thus have been one employed at a mill to sift meal or flour prior to its being bagged.

Sprout Waldron rollers at work in a small family mill in Delaware.

Three miller's offices. Although two are in commercial mills and one was a custom mill, they are very alike. Frequently the miller had his small office tacked onto the side of the main structure or pushed into a corner. They give the impression of business-only, and not places for conversation with visitors. Above is Jim Young's office at Wade's Mill, in Virginia, given over to labeling the paper bags for the mill's wide product range. On the right is the added-on wooden office at the side of Stephen Kindig's stone mill, in Lobachsville, Pennsylvania, left as it was last used. Below is the office at Rohrer's Mill, illustrating four generations of continuous use, everything in its place, like the rest of the mill, in positions formed by efficient habits.

"*It was a long and narrow building with a track of two wooden rails down its center. Along this track slid the carriage holding the log to be sawed. The saw itself was near the middle of the mill, which hence had to be about twice the length of the longest log sawed. The straight steel saw, with quite coarse teeth was some six feet long, stretched tight in a wooden frame which slide up and down between two so-called 'fender posts' grooved to receive the saw frame. Directly below the saw was the waterwheel which drove it . . . experience had shown that the saw should slide up and down about 120 times a minute.*"
The Village Mill in Early New England *by* Edward P. Hamilton

Sawmills

Germans claim that they invented the sawmill around 350 A.D. and the gristmill in 1389. Why they left these claims so late in the history of common experience is surprising, considering that the English Domesday Book of 1086 records 7,500 water-powered mills. But they may be right; certainly the British settlers in North America were slow in adapting the abundant sources of power around them. The first sawmills arrived in the 1670s. At mill seats, running a gristmill and a sawmill, millers preferred to separate them at least by a wall, or have the sides of the sawmill open to the elements. This gave them some protection from the risk of fire.

The early sawmill was really water power applied to a pitsaw. The up-and-down saw was a slender contraption attached to a beam, which joined a crank on the waterwheel. The saw went up and down within a frame that held it steady. The log to be sawn was drawn slowly, held on a long carriage operated by cogs, toward the blade.

An early sawmill could deliver a thousand feet of boards a day, which seems respectable, but was quickly regarded as a slow-motion, even leisurely, activity. A sawyer set the log, ran the saw, went and did something else, and came back in a while to inspect the progress.

The arrival of the circular saw eliminated the slow-moving crank, drawing its power directly from the wheel or turbine, and was much faster. Its hard steel blade made a finer cut, and saw more timber with less sawdust, but needed watching.

The circular saw at Rohrer's Mill awaits repair.

George Woodbury's *John Goffes's Mill* is a classic account of painstakingly restoring a sawmill-cum-gristmill. Here the author describes it running again: "The saw itself, a polished disc of steel armed with razor-sharp teeth, spins at truly terrifying speed. A circular mill saw running at appropriate speed would travel one hundred and twenty miles an hour were it in contact with the ground. No wonder the timbering and braces of a saw rig are so ponderous; no wonder the saw must be hung perfectly balanced and firmly bolted to the frame. The saw turns so fast it appears motionless, like a spinning top. The illusion is quickly dispelled as soon as the saw touches the log. The soft sibilance of the glistening plate changes to a demonic screech which rises and falls in tone as it parts clear wood, knots, or pitch pockets in the log. My ear became so attuned to the note that I could tell instantly the nature of the wood the saw was cutting, just by the quality of the scream."

Sawyers always kept to one side of the working saw, never in front of it; splinters or knots could shoot out at the speed of a bullet. Damage to the blade itself was the main concern. Experienced sawmill owners would not accept logs cut near a road or a house. They were almost certain to contain metal. Embedded hunters' bullets were an unknown risk but usually soft enough not to permanently damage the saw.

The up-and-down sawmill above is
powered by a flutter wheel. See the
Oliver Evans drawing on page 17.

118

Windmills

Woodchurch mill, in Kent, England.

The famous naturalist William Cobbett wrote over a century ago:
"The windmills on the hills in the vicinage are so numerous that I counted, while
standing in one place, no less than seventeen. They are all painted or washed white;
the sails are black. It was a fine morning, the wind was brisk, and their twirling
altogether added greatly to the beauty of the scene, which, having the broad and
beautiful arm of the sea on the one hand, and the field and meadows studded with
farmhouses on the other, appeared to me the most beautiful sight of the kind that I
had ever beheld."

*Nutley post windmill, the oldest
working windmill in Sussex, England,
dates from the late 17th century.*

Windmills were works of art, and no two mills were alike. Each was individually
made rather than mass produced. The windmill, which was always referred to as
"she" by the miller, usually took the name of the village it served. If not, then some
descriptive adjective or phrase, as in the case of the side-by-side Jack and Jill mills of
Clayton, Sussex in England, or the miller's name might be used. Although building a
windmill was carefully planned, until the mill was operating in place, no one could
know how effective it would be. Two mills too close together, for example, could set
up wind turbulence that would render each ineffective. A windmill was usually built
on a mound or a hill to catch the wind, but flat areas could also be used as long as
wind turbulence created by trees, buildings, or other mills could be avoided. Often
mounds were built specifically for the placement of a windmill. In addition to
grinding grain, mills served as a power source, but in areas where there were rivers
and streams, water mills took precedence. The exceptions were in Holland and East
Anglia, where wind power was used to move water. These windpumps looked exactly
like tower windmills and sometimes were used as gristmills, but their purpose was to
drain the fens and broads of England. In Holland, where they originated, it could be
said that they helped to build new areas of farmland by pushing back the inland sea.

*The Polegate brick tower windmill was
built in 1817 and restored to working
order in 1967.*

The design and operation of a windmill depended on various characteristics of the
wind, such as wind speed and changes in wind speed, wind direction and changes in
wind direction, wind turbulence, and the height of the wind above the ground. An
average windspeed of fifteen to twenty-five miles per hour and a prevailing wind
were necessary for operating a mill. The critical component of a mill's operation was
the sails. The force of the wind on the sails caused them to turn and rotate the axle,
or windshaft, on which they were set. The brake wheel, located inside the top of the
mill, was also attached to the windshaft, and its movement drove the millstones and
all other machinery inside the mill.

Mills usually had four sails, but five-, six-, and eight-sailed mills were also built. The
earliest sails were wooden, cloth-covered frames known as common sails. They were
light and powerful but had to be stopped for the miller to furl the sails. As windmill
design advanced, the cloth sails were replaced with sails with shutters. In 1807,
William Cubitt invented a sail that could be adjusted while the sails were turning.
The shutters of this sail could be opened and closed automatically and worked like
venetian blinds to aid in utilizing the wind. A windmill's sails always had to be
square into the "eye of the wind," since the mill was designed and balanced to resist
pressure from the front only. If a mill was tailwinded, the cloths or shutters could be
blown out, the cap blown off, or the mill itself blown over, often with the miller in it.
Because the wind changes, the mill had to be capable of being turned into the wind
whatever its direction.

*The Chailey smock mill has
been moved three times since
it was built in 1864.*

There are two general types of windmills: the post mill, in which the body of the mill
was turned into the wind, and the tower mill, in which the top, or cap was turned.

The post windmill in Williamsburg, Virginia.

Post Mills

If one described an old post windmill without the benefit of its image it would sound ridiculous. A tall box perched on cross-trees surrounding a thick post with four large blades on one side. The whole apparatus would have to be swiveled around into the wind by man, beast, or cartwheel. But when seeing it on the horizon, we translate its appearance into something fine, even beautiful.

The post mill is the earliest of windmills and is rare in North America; those that still exist are rebuilt or reconstructed. Because it is raised above ground it has a light, floating appearance. This impression is emphasized because the breast and the tail of the body are narrower than the sides, so that they may catch as little wind as possible. The mill post, sturdier than the village maypole, was a convenient symbol for all that was over-large in country life. It gave rise to sayings such as: "He hath thwittled the millpost of his huge conceit to the size of a pudding-pricke," and "his millpost legs are well adapted for the load of his body."

A view of Jill windmill from Jack. Both are situated in the village of Clayton, Sussex.

Robertson's windmill, in Williamsburg, Virginia, has its sails ready to turn.

The miller would put his shoulder to the tailpole and the well-greased wheel would turn the mill into the wind.

Common sails. The canvas or linen sheets were tied to the frames.

Colonial Williamsburg's William Robertson, clerk of the colony's council in 1698 and a city alderman by 1722, also operated a windmill.

Reconstructed on the original site, the post mill in Williamsburg is a replica of England's oldest post mill at Bourn, in Cambridgeshire, dating from 1636. The shape is medieval, with a steeply pitched roof, and its silhouette differs little from thirteenth century illustrations. Robertson's mill has common sails. The linen sails are spread over 26-foot-long, trellis-like frames, and when being set requires the work of three men. Two men climb up the sail framework to spread and secure the canvas, while a third operates the brake wheel. This activity takes about half an hour, and taking advantage of a windy day, it can be dangerous work. When the wind rose (a twenty- to thirty-mile-per-hour breeze was best), keeping everything running smoothly was tricky and dangerous. The running stone had to turn from 105 to 110 times a minute. For his trouble, the miller got a sixth of what he ground. For whatever it may say about Robertson's profits, he sold his windmill and four city lots to Mayor John Holloway in 1723 for a modest eighty pounds.

Mountnessing post mill, in Essex, England.

High Salvington post mill, in Sussex, England.

The body of a post mill is raised a considerable distance above the ground, for the sails should have a certain length if they are to reach well into the sky and catch sufficient wind. The wind pressure not only drives the sails around, but also exerts a rearward pressure on the sails and thus on the whole body of the mill. This pressure is taken mainly by the post, aided by the tail construction. At the rear of the mill a broad, oaken ladder descends from the body to the ground; there is also a heavy tail pole which, being connected to the framework of the floor of the wooden body, extends backwards from there. This tail pole passes between two rungs of the ladder and then curves slightly downward, while its end is firmly fastened to the end of the ladder by two upright oaken posts. At the bottom of the ladder, the winch or the winding wheel can be operated. This heavily constructed system of ladder and posts forms a counterweight for the great weight of the stocks with the sails, so that everything is balanced. When the mill is working, the ladder with the tail structure may rest on the ground and thus take the pressure of the wind on the sails and the mill body. The mill body can be reached from the ground along the ladder.

As they evolved, post mills gradually changed their appearance from the style shown on the preceding pages. The crosstrees became enclosed in a round house and the roofs began to curve, all the better to accommodate the large brake wheel.

Mountnessing post mill, in Essex, seen above left, is a good example of a narrow mill body giving the sails the most wind. High Salvington post mill, in Sussex, seen above, was built in the early 1700's and stopped working in 1900. After years when only its round house was in use as a tea room, the mill underwent restoration between 1976 and 1993. It is now in working order. A particular feature of this mill is its very large brake wheel, made with 111 cogs and three species of wood that interact with each other and maintain stability.

On the right is Jill of Clayton in Sussex, the companion to Jack. See the photograph on page 125, and the description on page 242. Although the stone floor is slowly sinking, she is restored to working order and grinds on special occasions. Like some other post mills she has moved; the last time to this site, in 1856.

Jill windmill arrived at this site in 1852.

Argos Hill post mill in Sussex, was built
in 1835 and stopped working in 1929.
It has a unique shape made by an
extension at the rear of the body, giving
the miller an extra four feet of space.
In one corner near the door was where he
had his tiny office.

Like another mill in the area, it has an
impressive tail-pole fan-tail. By 1956 the
mill was in bad condition and was a
dangerous structure. Since then it has
been gradually stabilized and made safe
for visitors. Although no longer able to
turn or work, the mill's original
machinery is intact, and there is an
impressive collection of milling
equipment arranged in the roundhouse.

Mountnessing miller Dusty Agnis, the last full-time miller at this Essex post mill, kept it in fine shape. He installed two hedgehogs in the roundhouse to prey on insects that were attracted to the grain, and hung thin strips of metal outside his bedroom window to wake him if the wind got up in the night. He would then rise, turn the mill into the wind, and get the sails turning.

After disuse and then coming into the hands of the parish council, the mill was sold to the county of Essex for the nominal sum of one shilling. Local citizens, concerned for the future of the mill, felt that the best way to preserve it was to restore the mill to full working order. They raised money with volunteer support, and with some financial help from the county, and a master millwright who lived in the next village, restored it part by part to get the mill turning. One
of the schemes was to "buy a shutter" for the spring sails at five pounds each. In 1983 the mill was officially reopened and set in motion.

The sharp-eyed observer will notice that windmill sails, apart from being angled, have a very slight twist to them. An inventor came up with a design that later enabled airplanes to fly. He discovered that if the four vanes, or sails, were fixed on the end of a spindle and pointed into the wind, they would revolve if each individual vane were twisted a little edgeways out of the wind. Experiments carried out by John Smeaton in 1759 determined that the best angles for the "weather" of the sail, were those that varied from approximately eighteen degrees at the heel to seven degrees at the tip, thus giving the sail the sort of twist that is seen in a propeller blade.

Common sails were very powerful and gained a lot of energy from the wind, but they had a big disadvantage. When the wind strength increased and the mill was running too fast, the miller had to trim the amount of canvas set by braking and stopping the mill. If the wind gusted powerfully he could have been in trouble; the mill turning so rapidly that the brake couldn't hold it. Out of control, the machinery might become damaged and at worst the sails may disintegrate, destroying much of the mill as they did so.

In 1772, Andrew Meikle, of England, invented a spring sail. This consisted of a number of hinged shutters in the sailframe. These were connected with a bar and the movement of the bar was controlled by a spring. The tension of the spring could be varied by adjusting a device at the tip of the sail, to permit a determined wind pressure. After the adjustment was made the action of the sail became automatic and the sails regulated themselves. They were never as strong as the common sails, but the miller had more control.

To overcome the disadvantage of adjusting a spring sail, in 1807, William Cubitt, a miller's son, brought out his "patent sail." A hole was drilled through the great axle of the windshaft that carried the sails. A rod, called the striking rod, passed through this hole and was connected to all the sail bars. The shutters were controlled by it with levers and spider coupling. On the other end of the striking rod was a toothed rack. This engaged a small pinion mounted on a common spindle with a chain wheel. Over this wheel an endless chain hung down either to a gallery or to the ground. Weights were hung on the chain, causing the shutters in the sails to remain closed until the wind pressure was sufficiently great to raise them. These weights could be altered at will without stopping the mill. This, together with improved cast-iron techniques, meant that taller and more powerful mills could be built.

Miller's Signals

When the day's milling is done, the miller disengages the stone nuts from the great spur wheel. He can then turn the sails to bring each one in turn down to the gallery. The shutters on the spring sails are opened to allow the wind to blow through. The canvas on the common sails is tightly rolled up and tied off along the length of the sail. The sails are then turned a little farther until they are in the diagonal position, and the brake applied. In this position the strain on the sails is equalized and the rain tends to run off the ends of the sails and fall clear of the gallery.

When the mill was closed, the miller was very careful to leave the sails set in the configuration of a St.Andrews cross, as this position left the sails balanced and afforded the least amount of strain. The position in which the sails were left could also convey messages to the people of the area. Shutters were removed for mourning—when more shutters were removed, the closer the relationship of the deceased. In some areas, lanterns were put on windmills to convey signals to smugglers. The illustrations on the right show various messages sent by sail positions.

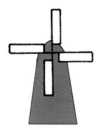

St. George's Cross: back soon

Mourning.

Celebration.

St Andrew's Cross: gone for the day.

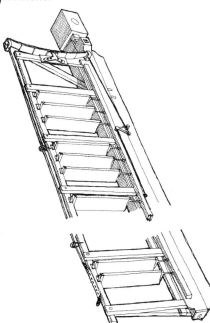

A section of a spring sail from Mountnessing windmill.

Tower Mills

The windmill in Orleans, Massachusetts, is a smock version of a tower mill.

The tower mill emerged in the middle of the sixteenth century in the Low Countries. Turning the whole mill around had been a cumbersome business, and in the relatively small space inside the post mill there was little room for storage, so loading and unloading always had to take place in the open. Post mills then evolved in the direction of the larger mills in which the body of the mill remained fixed, and the top, or cap, turned alone, carrying the windshaft with its sails and gearing. The cap revolved on blocks or rollers on a track or kerb. These early caps also had to be turned by hand, sometimes by means of long poles that reached almost to the ground. This method is still used in Holland today. Other caps were turned by means of a chain wheel, over which ran an endless chain or rope. This wheel was connected through suitable reduction gearing to a rack, so that when the chain was pulled the cap revolved.

Denver windmill, in Norfolk, England.

Burnham Overy tower mill.

There are two main types of tower mill. Built of stone or brick and circular in shape, it was called a tower mill. If built of wood—it had from six to twelve sides, the usual number being eight—it was called a smock mill, given its resemblance to the old-fashioned linen smock worn by laborers. A smock mill usually stands on a brick base. Some of them are built over this brick base, while others have been raised on to it to give them more height. Round the top of the brick base a wooden gallery or stage was often built to enable the miller to get at his sails more easily. This stage occurs on tower mills as well. A gallery round the cap was also frequently built.

The tarred-brick tower mill at Burnham Overy, in Norfolk, England, was raised in 1816. It remained in the family of its builder for eighty-five years; nineteen years later, after it was tailwinded, it finally stopped working, its machinery was removed, and was converted into a residence. Then, surprisingly, after it was given to the National Trust, there was a move to partially restore the mill, to get its cap to turn, and restore the winding gear, allowing the sails to revolve. The Trust came up against a bureaucratic snag when the County of Norfolk directed a refusal against the plan on the grounds that the local roads could not cope with the number of expected visitors!

The Working of a Tower Gristmill

Fantail

The Cap

The machinery in the cap is the most complicated part of a windmill. It does three quite separate things; first, when the sails are turned by the wind the upright shaft turns with them, which drives the millstones below. Second, the whole of the cap, bearing the sails and all the machinery, turns on top of the tower as the wind changes direction, rather like a huge weather vane.

Stocks

Sails

The Main Shaft

Stone floor

The stone floor is the heart of the mill where the wheat is ground into flour. The floor contains the two pairs of stones enclosed in their wooden vats, and spouts leading from the floor above lead into the center of the stones. There are a number of controls to regulate the speed of flow of the grain into the middle of the stones.

Spout floor

The spout floor is the last working floor of the mill, as the ground floor acts as an office and store for the miller. The main shaft is bedded on a beam just below the great spur wheel. The stone nut engages with the spur wheel and drives the stone shaft on which it is centered. The top of the stone shaft carries the spindle, on which the runner stone is supported. The flour from the stones travels down the spout to this floor and is collected in sacks.

*Barnham windmill,
as it looked
before restoration.*

Barnham Mill in 1900.

The tea room.

Barnham Tower Mill, in Sussex, England is being restored to the state it was when it prospered over a hundred years ago. The work is being carried out by its new owners, friends, and supporters.

Barnham Windmill was built in 1829 by the millwright Henry Martin to replace the post mill that had blown down on the night of Thursday, October 11, 1827. The tower mill was occupied in 1841 by George New and his wife, Anne. George New died on May 25, 1843, at age 32, of tuberculosis caused by miller's lung, brought on by the dusty conditions of the mill. The mill stopped using wind power by 1919 and carried on with a forty horsepower engine. By September 1939, at the beginning of the war with Germany, the sweeps (in southeastern England, this is the term for sails) had deteriorated and were removed. The mill was used as an observation post to alert RAF Tangmere of the approach of enemy aircraft. In 1985, under electric power, the mill produced animal feed, until it was put up for sale. In 1994, after an unsuccessful attempt at restoration, the mill was sold again.

Barry and Joy Lee became the new owners of the mill and attached buildings at the end of 1994. Their aim was to restore the Grade II-listed building to working condition and to grind wheat for demonstrations and for sale. They also planned to use the mill facilities for educational purposes. Work on the buildings progressed quickly and public tea-rooms were opened on July 8, 1995.

During the first six months, there were timber repairs and replastering for the interior. On the exterior, the copper cap was rubbed down and given a fresh coat of paint. The iron canister where the sweeps pass through was painted red, as was the new finial, which has been fitted at the top of the mill. The purpose of the finial was to allow the miller to place a rope around it, from which a bosun's chair was hung in order to carry out repairs to the tower.

The thoroughly renovated cap, together with the rebuilt fantail, was lifted into position by crane. Work on the cap had taken about one and a half years to complete. The copper sheeting dating back to 1958 has been replaced by lead, which is what originally covered the cap. The canister, finial, and fan star have been painted red—the authentic 1890 colors. The cast-iron curb was in sound condition and only needed wire brushing and greasing, revealing a feature on the curb marked in Roman numerals at the end of each section. Attention has now been given to getting the cap to become self-winding, and preparations are in hand for making the sweeps.

The tarred, weatherboarded smock mill at Sarre in Kent, England, shown on the left, has a post-mill cap turned by an eight-vane fantail, and carries four white patent sweeps driving two pairs of stones—a pair of French burrs and one of Peak gritstone. The mill stands on a two-story, tarred-brick base which had been raised one story in around 1856. It was built in 1820 and had a steam engine installed, possibly around 1856 when it was raised, and is said to be the first steam power installed in a Kentish mill. It continued working by steam, though it stopped using wind power in 1920, and finally ceased work in the 1930s. The mill was allowed to deteriorate, only being used briefly during World War II as an observation post. It was in poor condition when it was bought in the mid-1980s by the Hobbs family, who were descended from one of the early millers.

Father and son set about its complete restoration privately. The brickwork of the base was first tackled, then the structural woodwork. The weatherboarding has been renewed completely, the windshaft has been refurbished, a new cap built, and a new curb has been fitted. Most of the original machinery has also been restored. The mill has now been fully restored to work by wind, and grinds regularly on a commercial basis. It is open 364 days a year.

Right
Shipley Mill was built in 1879 (by a Mr. Grist) and is therefore the youngest of the Sussex smock mills and is still at work. It is a very modern mill with much iron machinery. The mill and the surrounding land was purchased by the writer Hillaire Belloc in 1906. Belloc died in 1953 and is buried at the Catholic church at West Grinstead. A plaque in his memory can be seen above the door of the mill.

The Smock Mill

The seventeenth-century smock mill, the last of the three main types to develop, is a variation on the tower mill. It was usually an octagonal, wooden structure with sloping, horizontally weatherboarded sides which resembled a countryman's linen smock from which its name derived. The mill was usually painted white or tarred black and often was set on a brick base to better catch the wind. The corners of the mill were protected with a strip of lead or zinc. However, weatherproofing was always a problem as rain drove through the joints, at the corners, and around the windows and doors. This type of mill suffered the most from weather damage. Sometimes the mill would have a gallery built around the cap. As in the case of the tower mill, only a smock mill's cap rotated to face the sails into the wind.

A thorough restoration of Shipley Mill was financed by Belloc's friends as a memorial to the writer. The stocks were replaced, and repairs carried out to the cant post, sails, cap frame, and boarding.

This Eastham windmill is believed to be the oldest on Cape Cod. This old mill was probably built in the early 1680s in Plymouth. Then it was taken across the bay to Provincetown in the late 1700s. In 1793, it was brought by road to Eastham, and then moved to its current location on Samoset Road in about 1808.

The mill on the green is very much the the center of life in the village. Every summer, Jim Owens, the illustrator and miller, can be found instructing tourists in the history and operation of the mill. In the fall, the residents of Eastham celebrate Windmill Weekend with a parade and activities on Windmill Green.

Looking up at the brake wheel in Eastham Windmill.

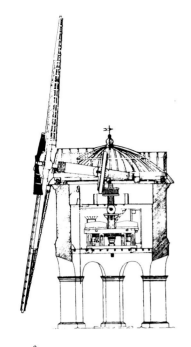

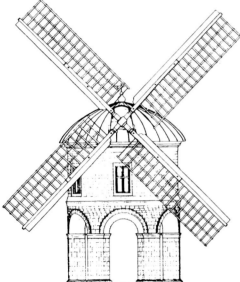

*Two views of
Chesterton windmill.*

*A section of the
Newport tower windmill.1*

Any deviation from the familiar windmill form has given rise to thoughts that it might be something other than just a mill. Derek Ogden, the distinguished millwright, would find few to disagree with his opinion that Chesterton Windmill is the most beautiful windmill to be seen anywhere.

It is widely believed that the classical stone structure was designed by Inigo Jones (1573–1652) the famous seventeenth-century architect, who first brought the Palladian principles to Britain with his designs for the Queen's House at Greenwich, Whitehall Palace, and St. Paul's Covent Garden. As the first owner of Chesterton was known to be proficient in mathematics and a student of astronomy, some thought that such an elegant "building" must have been an observatory. It is more likely the client's love of architecture was the only reason for its appearance. Documentary evidence dating from 1647 proves that she has always been a windmill.

In Newport, Rhode Island, there had been attempts over the years to prove that a similar, though much less well-built structure, had not been a windmill. This was known as the Norse Theory: that Vikings had settled in Newport and had built some sort of round church. The features of the two towers are quite similar, but the one in Newport differs in two areas. It is built of unworked native stone and rests upon eight round pillars. Chesterton is built of finely worked limestone and has six ornamental pillars.

The Newport Tower no longer retains its cap, machinery, or floors. Some scholars and many others had claimed the tower to be of Viking origin, but this has been proved incorrect. The site was excavated in 1948 and 1949, when over 20,000 artifacts dating to the Colonial period were removed. A scientific dating process has recently confirmed a Colonial date for the tower. Samples were taken in 1993 in a variety of places and from a depth where "pollution" from repair work could be excluded. These were tested and showed that the tower was probably built in the middle of the seventeenth century.

Derek Ogden, who restored the machinery at Chesterton, wrote in *Old Mill News* that "the theory which has survived is that the Newport mill was constructed by Governor Arnold from his memory of Chesterton Windmill. Arnold was born in Somerset, England, and like many other travelers, probably journeyed along the Fosse Way with his family. As a teenager, he would have been impressed by the incredible beauty of the newly completed mill at Chesterton. When his earlier post mill at Newport blew down in the great hurricane of 1675, he replaced it with a more substantial tower, like the one he had seen at Chesterton."

The smock windmill in Jamestown, Rhode Island.

Windmills were never as numerous as watermills in America and were
restricted to areas around New York, such as Long Island, New Jersey,
eastern Rhode Island, Nantucket, Cape Cod, and similar places where strong
ocean breezes and unobstructed open space provided the necessary wind
force. In these areas streams were limited in force or affected by tides—a
disadvantage to waterwheel mills. Water-powered mills were also subject to
droughts, flooding, freezing, and the destructive action of water on wood.
There were a number of wind-powered sawmills, but as farms continued to
grow, more gristmills began to open. They are smock mills, usually
octagonal, cant-framed, and shingle-covered. Their caps are what distinguish
individual mills.

*The Corwith mill, in the village of Watermill, Long Island, made her way to this
spot, drawn by a team of oxen in 1814.*

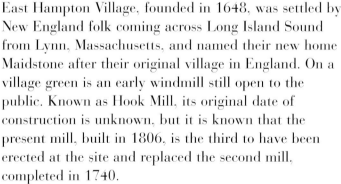

East Hampton Village, founded in 1648, was settled by New England folk coming across Long Island Sound from Lynn, Massachusetts, and named their new home Maidstone after their original village in England. On a village green is an early windmill still open to the public. Known as Hook Mill, its original date of construction is unknown, but it is known that the present mill, built in 1806, is the third to have been erected at the site and replaced the second mill, completed in 1740.

Nathaniel Dominy, a local millwright is credited with the building and others in the region. The Dominy family was involved in building and operating windmills in the eastern Long Island area for generations. As late as 1942, Charles Dominy operated the Hook Mill, which was built by his great-great-grandfather.

A few hundred yards away is Pantigo Mill, built in 1804, and operated for seventy years. At the turn of the twentieth century, damaged after a hurricane, Nathaniel Dominy V's wife turned the mill into a rather primitive tourist accommodation, when the sail-less hulk became known to early "Hamptons" tourists as "Venus de Millo." In 1916 it was moved to become a museum on the grounds of the saltbox cottage where John Howard Payne was born and inspired to write the song "Home Sweet Home."

The move proved to be the the windmill's saving when, in 1977, it was being demolished by carpenter ants. Payne's birthplace was thought worthy enough to be entered in the National Register of Historic Places. The mill was included, making it eligible for restoration funds.

Miller's Tales

Over the years there have been many accounts of the day-to-day events of life in a gristmill, and not a few about the adventures in the often risky business of milling. As I have said before, millers and almost certainly millwrights were, and are, versatile people. They needed to be, for the mill in their charge had huge iron and wooden machinery to be manhandled, and delicate berries of wheat needed just the right touch. Windmills were particularly demanding, requiring a head for heights and an eye for the weather. Today, when mills are restored they all carry lightning conductors. Windmills standing on their chosen high ground have been hit time after time by thunderbolts. Here is a selection of stormy miller's tales.

The chains for turning the sails into the wind or hoisting sacks ran down from the top to the bottom of the mill and spread the voltage:
"The sack chain was once welded solid when the mill [Farndon] was struck by lightning...On one occasion lightning cut the weight chain and the weights, chain and all fell through the wash-house roof." *Rex Wailes*

"The electric fluid now became concentrated in the chain that was used for drawing up the sacks; this was in part fused, as the links were welded together in one solid mass. The good effect of the conducting power of the chain was very perceptible, as little or no damage was done in that section of the mill through which that part of the chain passed. By this chain the ethereal fire entered the lower compartment, and was diverted from its downward course by some half-hundred and other weights standing on the floor near the western side of the mill; here it tore up a large space of the floor, the weights were ejected into the yard to a considerable distance, and the boards were forced off as before with great violence, and thrown in every direction."
The miller survived:
"Apparently insensible of pain, and regardless of the injuries he had sustained, his first enquiry was as to the state of the mill and the corn. When the spectators had recovered from the alarm excited by the mutilated appearance of the sufferer, they conveyed him to a house and the assistance of a surgeon was speedily obtained. Upon further examinations, large splinters of wood, and even grains of wheat from the hopper were found driven into various parts of his body."— *Chelmsford Chronicle, 1829*

"One of the sails was split in two or three places, the wooden roof ripped open, a massive wooden roller rent into fragments, gas piping torn away and the silks of the dressing machines burnt to ashes. On the ground floor the gas meter was lifted up and hurled through one of the windows, tearing away the woodwork along with it. Mr Longbottom was there at work. His hair as well as the whiskers on one side was burnt off and his face skinned. He was much shaken and had to take to his bed." *The Miller, 1885*

Sutton windmill is Britain's tallest windmill and a famous Norfolk landmark. The historic corn mill was built over two hundred years ago, and was in use until 1940. Restoration work is still in progress while it is open to the public. A policy of traditional replacement is being pursued, using materials as near to the original as possible.

Sutton, like other brick tower mills, has windows one above the other. The brick wall rises unbroken from foundation to cap, giving strength. Yet some millwrights, seeing mills that had lines of windows with vertical cracking from top to bottom of the tower, built their mills with windows in a spiral, looking out in a different direction from each floor.

Suzanne Beedell, in *Windmills*, records a twentieth-century near-accident:
"It was about 3:30 in the afternoon and I didn't like the look of the sky. The mill had been working with the wind in the southeast, but the wind dropped right away. I struck up the mill at once and chained the striking bar to the fly post. While I was doing this there came a little air from the north. . .The fly ran, and got back as far as northeast and stopped. By this time I could see a great cloud approaching from the west, accompanied by sheet lightning and rolling thunder. As I was up with the fly I had a good view over the surrounding countryside and could see the direction and speed of the approaching storm. I hastily turned the fly by hand and had nearly got the mill back to north when the gale hit her. I moved inside the mill very quickly. . .I had never seen a fly go so fast, nor have I since. She raced into the storm and went dead west, then two minutes later went back to the north. The storm eased later and the wind returned to the west and began to lull, but had I not turned the fly by hand as I did she would have been tail winded and the top of the mill would have been blown off. This storm was the worst I ever experienced."

Two accounts from Norfolk mills:

"The whole mill rocked so that the sacks of grain. . .were thrown down like paper, but I got the brake lever somehow and threw all my weight on it, but it hardly seemed to check her. I knew that if the brake was kept on she was bound to catch fire, so I left off, and round she went, running at such a rate that the corn flew over the top and smoke blinded and suffocated me."

"The lightning passed down the windshaft, riving the timbers and dislodging the opposite sail completely. . .The damage to the crown, brake wheel, wallower, and other gear was tremendous and the whole of the roof was flung off. . .The miller was found maimed and blackened and one leg had to be amputated. Splinters of wood and grains of wheat had penetrated his skin, and during the months of convalescence, more than and cupful of grain was extracted."

The miller's greatest fear was fire:

On January 15th the windmill on Clarborough Hill, at Retford, caught fire. The local fire brigade was quickly on the spot, but nothing could be done to save the building, which was totally destroyed. The fire originated through the friction caused by the gale which released the grips, and drove the sails round with immense velocity.—*The Miller*, 1896

Machinery could catch the unwary miller. Nineteenth century journals had many long descriptive accounts of such accidents (invariably fatal) that would never be published today. Here is a less terrifying report:
"On the afternoon of Saturday last, Mr. Cross of Worstead, Miller, met with a most distressing accident. The flyers of his mill not being in working order, he and his men ascended to put them right and whilst doing what was wanted, it being dark at the time, the clothes of Mr. Cross were caught and he was drawn into the machinery, and we are sorry to report that one of his legs was so mangled that amputation was inevitable. His other leg was also broken in three places but has since been set, and although great fears have been entertained of his surviving the shock, we learn that he is better than could be expected."—

Forty miles from the sea, the tower of a Norfolk windpump becomes a home with the cap area converted to a lighthouse-like observartory.

Sometimes one had to look out:

A fatal accident happened on Thursday the 1st, to a youth named James Crampton, in the employ of Mr. Oldham, miller, Newark. He was told by his master to go down into the roundhouse, but instead of descending the stairs he walked upon the platform erected for adjusting the sails and proceeded to jump down, when one of the sails struck him upon the head. He died shortly afterward.—*Stamford Mercury*, 1854

Stanley Freese, in *Windmills and Millwrighting*, said that "tales are sometimes told of millers 'going round on the sails' while they were running, but I have found that even windmill enthusiasts sometimes disbelieve these stories. I therefore wish to state categorically that I have met several millers and former mill boys who went round on the sails in days gone by. They thought little of it because they often climbed the sails to do repairs and make adjustments."

In 1807, it was reported that "a clergyman indicted a miller for working his mill so near the common highway as to endanger life. The clergyman is a man of considerable property and consequence in the county. He was obliged daily to pass by this road on horseback, and has been several times thrown by his horse taking fright at the sails of the mill." The Court resolved that rather than urge the vicar to get a properly broken-in horse, it was easier to pay the miller forty pounds as an incentive to move his mill.

Stephen Kindig, in a past issue of *Old Mill News*, supplied the following anecdote extracted from a copy of *Practical Hints on Millbuilding*, published in 1880. It concerns the people from the Hutzelwald area in Germany, who were inclined to be rather slow and averse to change.

"Well, these people decided to build a mill. They quarried and cut a millstone from the hill, three hundred feet above the mill site, and were at a loss to know how to get it down. They decided to let it roll down, but, unfortunately, it turned to the left, and ran down a ravine. After several days diligent search they found it in a thicket, one and a half miles from the mill. Simply recognizing that the blunder was made in not giving it a proper start, they, with great difficulty, carried it to the top of the hill from which it was started. Lest it be lost again one of the party put his head through the eye of the stone, intending to accompany it down the hill in this manner, and in case it departed from the intended course, he promised to whistle, that the others might find it. Hannes (who in his young days had been hostler in an artillery corps), with the air of a military expert, proceeded to make a reconnaissance of the field and aimed the stone directly for the mill door, gave the command, 'fire!' and off they let it go. The weight of a man on one side, of course, caused the stone to rapidly change its course, and man and stone went crashing through bushes and trees, finally landing at the bottom of a small lake. The parties on the hill vainly waited for a signal—and vainly searched for the stone. After carefully considering the matter, they concluded that the man, knowing the stone was of considerable value, had run away with it. Therefore the burgermeister was authorized to publish the following: 'Reward!!! Five thalers vil becomen to de man as vil arrest eine deutschman mit eine mill shtone arount mit his head.'"

Looking up to the fantail stage of the Stracey Arms windpump.

The task of turning a post mill, or the cap of a tower or smock mill, with tail pole or chain was gradually eliminated after 1745, when Edmund Lee patented a device that faced the mill into the wind automatically. His circular fantail, or fly tackle, was a small windmill with wooden slanted blades, mounted behind the cap, or near the ground at the end of the tailpole, at right angles to the sails. A shaft from its axle transferred its motion through a series of gears. The biggest gear, fixed to the cap, turned the smaller gear, below which meshed with cogs around the base of the cap. Spun by the wind, it pulled the cap around to the right position. As the sails began to turn, the fantail remained idle in the dead air behind the mill until a gust of wind turned the blades. Its gear ratio was so high that it could turn an entire post mill like the one shown on pages 132–133.

Drainage Mills

Holland owes its creation as well as its development in the most literal sense to the windmills, or, more accurately, windpumps. In the seventeenth century the Dutch made more and more progress in the fight against their foe, the water. The pumping windmill delivered the country of the water and kept it dry, despite the fact that most of the country lies several feet below sea level. It is a fight that continues to this day as what remains of the Zuyder Zee and the great polders are filled in and turned into rich farmland and room for the ever-growing population.

Across the North Sea, in Norfolk, mills were built to drain the Broads marshes—the flat, open landscape between Norwich and the east Norfolk coast. In Roman times this area was an estuary, covered by the sea at every high tide. Late in about the fifth or sixth century, the sea level gradually started to drop, land appeared, and plants began to grow. The Saxons embanked parts of the rivers to prevent further flooding and they used the land on either side for grazing cattle. At the end of the thirteenth century the sea level gradually started to rise. Since then, only careful embankment and drainage have prevented the area from being reclaimed by the sea.

The experienced Dutch drainage engineers were brought over to supervise the erection of many of the first Broadland mills, and by the end of the nineteenth century, there were over 240 mills. The only other parts of England that were drained in the same way were the fen areas of Cambridgeshire, Lincolnshire, and West Norfolk, where there were over one thousand mills. Few remain there now, and the Broads have the largest concentration of windmills in Britain.

Right
Thurne Windmill is known as the Lady Mill because her body is similar to a high-waisted, long-skirted dress. The beautifully curved lines of the mill body also have a practical purpose: the wind from the descending sail meets with less resistance.

In 1919, she was tailwinded and her sails and cap ended up in the marshes of Thurne Dyke. Now restored and leased to the Norfolk Windmills Trust, the windpump is open to the public throughout the summer.

A cutaway drawing of the Turf Fen Mill showing the double scoop wheel.

In the late-eighteenth century, drainage in Broadland was extended and the area became a landscape of drainage mills, which look like small windmills, but they lift water instead of grind corn. The water was lifted by scoop wheels out of the low-lying marsh ditches into higher-level embanked dykes and rivers, which eventually carried it out to sea at Great Yarmouth.

Turf Fen Mill was built by millwright William Rust around 1875 and is typical of the brick tower mills in the Broads. It has the Norfolk boat-shaped cap, six-bladed fantail, and four double-shuttered sails of seven bays each. An unusual feature is the double scoop wheel with a choice of high or low gears. It was used to drain Reedham Marshes and stopped working in the 1920s, when the marsh was no longer used for cattle. The Norfolk Windmills Trust took over responsibility for Turf Fen in 1976, and by 1986 major restoration work was complete, including a new cap and sails.

Drainage windpumps such as this one pumped the water from the dykes, which intersect and drain the land, into the Broads and tidal waterways. The Horsey windpump has been restored, and is owned by The National Trust and open to visitors. Its workings are interestingly described by the Trust: "An often easily understood analogy is that of the pump pumping water off a bathroom floor up into the bath and out through the plug hole into the sea. Water pumped at Horsey from the low-level system to the higher level reaches the sea at Great Yarmouth after a course of twenty-three miles. This watercourse is affected throughout its length by the tide in the North Sea. A southeast wind lets the water out. A north-west wind, in particular at full and new moon, holds the water up. Northeast and southwest winds are neutral."

Many of the Broadland windpumps and windmills have a distinctive cap, rather like an upturned clinker-built boat. This was introduced by a firm of millwrights and boat-builders at Ludham, in the heart of the Broads.

In the north of Holland the windpumps turn an Archimedian screw to raise water from the polder.

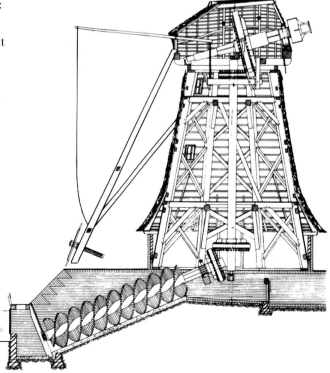

In 1854, Daniel Halladay invented a device that used wind for pumping groundwater. By 1860, his multibladed windmill pumper was proven to be a positive force in agriculture by tapping precious water sources from aquifers below the surface. Farmers enjoyed cheap and reliable sources of water for livestock and clean water for household consumption.

In the United States, the advent of rural electrification in the 1930s diminished the importance of windmill pumping technology and many were sold for scrap in World War II. Only on farms where the Amish shun any connection to electrical power supply do we see the once-familiar rural silhouette. Today, the looming threat of fossil fuel depletion, the creeping deserts in the Third World, and environmental awareness have reinstated the windmill as a possible energy source, especially for generating electricity. Towers of double- or triple-bladed "wind farms" that entrepreneurs are building on scenic ridges may change society's fond collective image of the windmill.

A New Life for Mills

Looking out over the millpond.

The flutter wheel at work.

Among the rural mills that survive in some form, a good number are being returned to full- or part-time use. Among these, as we have seen, there are examples where milling enthusiasts, historians, and educators have worked with state or local authorities to tell the story of natural power.

There are mills that were abandoned and have been saved for residential and other uses. Successful compromises are where the owners combine their lives with getting some of the mill working. They are responsible custodians for a structure that may be needed again for what it was intended. But some old water mills dried up, losing their source of power, which had been diverted or cut off by authorities or developers. Here the owners must be commended for at least saving the building.

The examples that follow illustrate the work of new owners who recognize the spirit of the mill and adapt their living and work styles to fit the structure. Old barns are a good match for those seeking open contemporary space. With mills, the owners have to be flexible. Here, the integrity of the building and the integrity of the owners combine to tell us about the past and future of naturally powered buildings.

All over the areas where water powered the Industrial Revolution, there are once busy, once abandoned, large industrial buildings, factories really, that are getting a new life as museums, outlet malls, offices, and apartments. When these large buildings were working at capacity, the small mills outside of town were finished, regarded as relics of the first settlers. At the end of the nineteenth century in the northeast, artists and writers moved into country mills, feeling that they would be at one with the elements, history, and arts and crafts.

The illustrations on the previous pages and these pages are of a mill in Connecticut that has been carefully restored to its original purpose as an operational up-and-down sawmill. It has also been adapted as a summer home, with accommodation on the upper level, and the sawmill floor as a living room. Both uses are separate, yet important in continuing the life of the mill.

Hank Browne is a restoration architect whose projects have included the governor's mansion in Richmond, five of Thomas Jefferson's buildings, the Lincoln Memorial, over thirty historic houses in Fredericksburg, and an Ulster farmhouse at the Museum of American Frontier Culture. Over the years he would drive by Walker's Mill in Albemarle County, Virginia. He knew that it suffered badly in the 1938 hurricane, which burst the millpond dam, and then stopped for good after 155 years of milling. It had been built in 1783, the first year of the new United States, and Jefferson, who lived nearby, was a familiar visitor. His Memorandum Book records, "*Set out for Washington. Pd. for corn at T Walkers mill.*"

The ruined mill as seen from the road.

Stage one, after cleaning up.

The gooseneck flume pipe collapsing on the waterwheel.

The original date stone.

After disuse the mill became a makeshift summer home, abandonment and its overgrown isolation led it to become a haven for vagrants and hippies. Browne, by now totally involved in saving historic buildings, was depressed by its state. "In my opinion, they all but trashed the place and nearly burned it down." He bought the mill as a derelict hulk nearly hidden behind a thicket of multiflora roses. The roof had rotted and one wall had caved in. It was ready for bulldozing. Browne began his personal challenge to save it and make it a home. Ever the historian and student, he recorded every state of the ruin, and began his reconstruction research by sketching every possibility of what had been there and what could be achieved as the remains were stabilized. Nine months later he concluded that all that could be retained were the three stone walls, the timber framing that was spanned above them, the wheel pit, and the stout eighteen-foot Fitz wheel. Another sadness was finding that vandals had chipped off the face of the original date stone that Mr. Walker built into the wall when the mill was ready.

The magnificent double doorway, minus its date stone.

The wheel pit after being dug out.

Compare with the image on the opposite page.

The return to the original roofline.

An impression of the mill ruin before final collapse.

The initial conjecture, and raising the roofline.

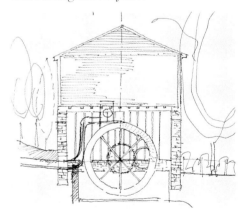

A mile-long sluiceway had fed the gooseneck pipe above the wheel.

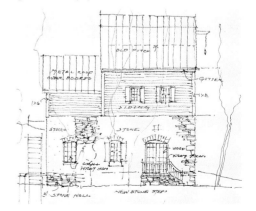

Approaching completion with the eighteen-foot wheel back in position.

Hank Browne noted that the mill's original roof had a much steeper pitch than the one stuck on in the 1950s. By examining the angles of the rafter slots in the original supporting plates and looking at the roof of another mill built by Thomas Walker's son, John, Browne found the correct angle.

Compare with the opposite page.

Original posts are stabilized before the stone floor is relaid.

The only window on one side was this flapped opening.

The idea was retained on a new section of the wall.

In the reconstruction, Hank Browne resolved to keep the original interior spaces and rebuilt a stairway to where the old landing had been. Respect for the building led him to design the mill's first conveniences and plumbing in a three-story conjectural addition. He could find no evidence of exactly what had stood there before.

What was once the main milling floor is now an open living room. Hank Browne's work on the Ulster farmstead led him to deduce that the masons who laid the stone floor were Scotch-Irish. The second floor and attic were built of hand-hewn beams, fastened with walnut pegs.

The new fireplace is tested on a cold day.

Before the mill was restored there was no plumbing. The narrow kitchen has its sink built into a deep recess of the only window in the original stone wall.

The 36-inch-thick stone walls were plastered with horsehair, lime, and mud from the creek—a finish Brown has replicated with a coat of stucco.

A mixture of angles in Hank Browne's stairway design lead up to the charred marks of a near disaster when the mill was being vandalized.

The original landing leads to the *L*-shaped second-floor study/bedroom. The fanlight above the bed brings borrowed light to the stairway leading to the third-floor studio. Browne has seen this in old mills before. With the risk of fire so real, millers would take pains not to use lamps and candles.

As a professional who has worked for many years saving worthwhile historic domestic and working buildings, and campaigning for their lives, Browne states that the new life for Walker's Mill is "not historic preservation…This just happened to be an old building that has been preserved and restored."

Could the mill work again? Probably not, but the wheel could turn again under water power. According to Hank Browne, the sluiceway works well, and if the old wooden sluice box is rebuilt, a recirculating pump would deliver water to the top of the wheel.

In 1985, Kenneth and Heather Parker fell in love with the eighteenth-century Maplehurst Mill and impulsively bought it. Their romantic feelings were then tempered by the problems of owning a disused agricultural building, which was habitable but needed lots of work. Their plan was to restore the mill's wheel and grinding machinery, but to do so, it needed to earn its keep, so they decided to turn the big grain-storage areas on the second and third floors into rooms for paying guests.

The Parkers were aware that this was a controversial decision since the purist approach would have been to leave the mill exactly as they found it, yet spend lots of money to keep it standing. However, they could not have taken it on under those circumstances. Their solution was to highlight the contrasts between what was originally there and the renovations, so it is easy to understand the history of the large white mill and timber-framed house, originally built in 1480 and subsequently enlarged.

On the first floor, the mill workings lie intact behind a wooden partition.

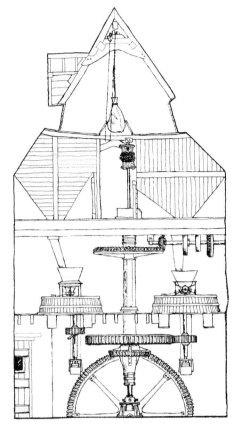

An English gristmill similar to the one described.

A new stairway leads to the grinding floor where, in the nineteenth-century section, the guest drawing room features the old smutter and scourer. On the top floor, the grain bins have been left in place, while two bedrooms have been created from the grain-storage space.

Throughout the interior, the original timbers remain, and new wood has been left unaged, presenting a contrast and following the old agricultural tradition of patching with new material.

The Parkers placed partition walls between the timbers of the existing structure, and no timbers were cut or hidden. One of the bedrooms even contains the cantilevered sack hoist in the ceiling. They carefully inserted new windows with those on the front and back, copying the size and structure of the original ones exactly, down to the internal hook-and-eye fastenings.

With these and other intelligent compromises, the Parkers have managed to preserve the mill and its integrity into the twenty-first century.

A converted mill in the country is a tranquil waterside escape from city life. It is difficult to imagine them as once noisy and busy. Until the 1930s, when it stopped working, there had been an active mill here in Hampshire, England, since the twelfth century. It consists of two adjoining buildings, the long mill proper, and the taller, mill owner's house.

The main activity at the mill today is the millrace, seen under two sections of the glass-tiled mill floor. Remaining is the control for a version of a Pelton wheel, a turbine made of a series of cups attached to a hub. A jet of water was aimed at the cups, and the resulting force caused the turbine to spin.

Once the main mill, the sitting room is divided by a
solid white fireplace. Salt-glazed Italian tiles provide
a common flooring, while the high-angled ceiling
allows ample space for a large collection of books.

Many of the old mills of France have a new life as hotels, restaurants, and vacation retreats. At one small part of the River Dronne, in Brantôme, two water mills cater for discerning visitors. Above, on its own island, Le Moulin Bateau has become a comfortable vacation home for rental; below, Le Moulin de l'Abbaye is renowned as a hotel with a restaurant that attracts diners from all over Europe.

The timber-framed Sherriff Mitchell Mill has been converted into a family home. Apart from the removal of a section of the second floor, there were few changes in the conversion. The owners kept the shafts and pulleys in place, and leaving the top ceiling structure exposed was an easy and honest solution to allow the additional workings to be seen.

The Sylvan Falls Mill site has been the location of a working gristmill for more than 150 years. The first mill was constructed in 1840 from wormy chestnut wood. The original, wooden waterwheel was replaced in 1946 by a 27-foot Fitz steel wheel moved from Tennessee. The waterfall, fed from the springs of Black Rock Mountain, cascades down one side of the property that overlooks the Wolffork Valley. The large red wheel turns easily and the flume is in good condition, fed from the dam farther up the mountain. Today, the mill is a comfortable bed-and-breakfast retreat in the northern Georgia mountains.

The red-painted waterwheel is a striking feature and can be seen from a distance.

The rich farmland and the streams running into the Susquehanna River made York County, Pennsylvania, home to many prosperous gristmills. Toward the end of the nineteenth century the mill at Clear Spring was rebuilt and enlarged. In 1886, a blacksmith shop, tannery, distillery, and general store clustered around the mill; business was booming and Edward Dick needed a larger mill. The stone foundation was extended, and the wooden overshot wheel was then protected inside the foundation. The simple, two-story pitched-roof structure was replaced with a full three stories under a mansard roof with some touches of country elegance in a version of the Second Empire architectural style. The operation included three runs of stones in the gristmill, and an additional run located in the sawmill, which was used for grinding limestone. Clear Spring was alive with activity.

But as times changed, what had been a thriving business in the 1880s was no longer profitable by the 1940s. Most of the iron and steel was sold to scrap mongers during and following World War II. In 1947, Clear Spring Mills ground its last sack of cornmeal, and this charming piece of rural history was left to fend for itself as best it could.

The mill became a giant catch-all farm shed. A huge hole was hacked in the back wall to move a hammermill inside. As time went on, the standing seams of the metal roof let loose one by one, and the beautiful fish-scale slate on the mansard roof began to deteriorate. The dormers started leaking at the joints. Window sills rotted away, while tree branches, pigeons, and vandals took their toll on the sashes. The Dutch doors were broken by vandals and repeatedly boarded up, using longer nails each time.

Finally, in 1980, the family descendants removed the millstones for momentoes and auctioned off the rest of what was left inside. Late in 1994, Art and Donna Bert acquired the gristmill, the sawmill ruins, and six acres of land.

The story of Clear Spring Mills today is about dedication to a landmark. Art and Donna Bert knew when they bought it that it could never be what it was. Defunct for nearly fifty years, the mill had been cut off from its original water by a new U.S. highway. They wanted to bring back what the mill represented: its role as a center in people's lives.

Donna, Art, and their two sons took on the tasks they were comfortable with. Cleaning the fifty-year accumulation of dirt and debris was just the start. Window sashes were repaired and reglazed, more than four hundred panes with beautiful, wavy old glass. Stairways and entrances were rebuilt. Rotting or missing window sills and thresholds were replaced. Finally, after checking through the layers of pigment and nearly fifty gallons of paint, the Berts have brought Clear Spring Mills back to the same exterior colors Edward Dick intended in 1886. In 1996, they received the Award of Excellence from the Pennsylvania Historic and Museum Commission for their work.

Two versions of the progress at Clear Spring. The mill floor just after the building was restored, and on the right, today as a fully functioning mill store, with its own granary products, books, and gifts that relate to history and local interest and many other items. Like Wade's Mill in Virginia, it has become a gathering place for social activities, weekend artisans' workshops, dinner theater, and concerts. Behind the mill, the Berts are building their new home, a restored Pennsylvania log farmhouse.

More recently they began restoration on what remained of the adjoining sawmill, which once got its power from the gristmill machinery. The second floor will be used as a woodworking shop and the first floor as a weaving studio.

195

In western Connecticut the rivers flow south into Long Island Sound. The area attracted more prospectors than farmers because the rocky soil held an abundance of resources that could be used by enterprising engineers and manufacturers. There was fast-moving water for power, plenty of hardwood for timber framing, rocks for foundations, enough limestone for cement and fluxing the most important resource, iron ore. Many forges and furnaces sprang up, with waterwheels pumping their bellows, as many sawmills, and tanning factories to supply leather belts for mill pulleys. New England was dug, carved, and blasted into business.

Riverdance Mill was once the site of the Watamaug Iron Company. In 1875, after years of mismanagement, the furnace was demolished. Its rocks were used to strengthen the former dam and became the foundation of a combined sawmill and general-purpose machine shop.

The mill, down in a narrow, shaded channel, has very large windows at each end. They gave much-needed light to aid the skilled activities inside—the factory built and finished carriages, with coachlines that had to be painted with long, narrow sable brushes. The work was carried out on the floor above the wood-turning machinery, raised and lowered by an elevator. Later, the windows illuminated the crafting of violins and cellos.

While writing *Early American Mills*, Martha and Murray Zimilies visited the mill as activities slowed:

"This lovely, barn-red mill is situated in the town of New Preston, Connecticut, on the East Aspetuck River. It was built on the site of an old iron furnace that operated as far back as the 1700s. In the Civil War period Oscar Beeman chose this spot to build a saw mill and carpentry shop.... Beeman was a local master builder; some of his barns can still be found in the surrounding area. They are recognized by their characteristic cupolas. The same techniques were used to build the barns here and at the mill. First the building's frame was erected. Then the sides, complete with windows, were constructed on the ground and raised into place by horses and men....To this day, winter or summer, wet or dry, his windows never stick....This is one of the beautiful mills that remains in the Northeast."

The boarded-up mill before restoration.

This detail shows the original timber frames and braces of the corner that rests on the stone wall shown on the left. Underneath was where the logs entered the the sawmill.

The cupola supports are found to be rotten.

The cupola is removed.

The rafters are replaced.

The existing frame is prepared for insulation.

Slates are laid on the roof, and the mill awaits clapboarding and the reinstallation of the cupola.

By the 1990s, empty and up for sale, the mill factory was in a bad way, sagging in one corner, the base of the cupola was rotting, and some of Oscar Beeman's large windows needed replacing.

Following the manner of Mr. Beeman, the new owners had no architect or drawings. They relied on the skills of a local builder who knew the history of the mill. With children attending local schools, their mother stayed in local accommodations, and worked every day with the craftsmen as the mill became the family home. She photographed every stage of the restoration, tagging machinery so that it could be kept in place, or adapted for reuse.

The repaired and reinstalled cupola brings light to an upper floor.

The original workings above the turbine.

As work progressed, there was the problem of access between floors; the carriage elevator was gone and there were only ladders. On a return visit from California, the husband suggested that the shaft up from the turbine and its frame could support a stairway. This proved to be a wonderful solution, enabling them to retain the machinery passing though three levels and framed by the turning stairs. Clear, laminated safety glass is fitted below the rails that surround the shaft.

The north end of the main floor. One of the owners discovered the heart-shaped keystone above the fireplace.

The master bedroom looks out onto the millpond.

As in the original, the main floor that once housed the milling
equipment is basically one space, save for the two massive sliding
doors that divide the dining area from the kitchen.

Pulley brackets are tagged for use as andirons.

The original mill had no plumbing. The outhouse was perched in the angle of the main structure and the narrow extension that housed the shaft and gears driven by the turbine below. It is now a tiled shower.

Right:
A pair of pulleys are now handles on the new front door.

The lower sawmill floor of Riverdance Mill. The massive chimney, like the supporting wall, was built by local masons from rocks on the site. The owners adapted shaft brackets as andirons. As restoration proceeded, they tried to retain any wood or metalwork that could be adapted to further use. In their efficient way the builders had begun to dispose of any nonconstruction items they found, and one of the owners had to tie red tags, or retrieve from the dumpster what became known between them as her "artyfacks."

The Gilbert Mill, in Avon, New York, is the only well-preserved eighteenth-century mill in the Genesee Valley. The mill site was cleared with the help of local Indians and the abundant timber was used to build a long-low gristmill that had a large rock shelf as part of the foundation.

In 1837, Charles, S. Gilbert, a twenty-year-old English miller's apprentice, emigrated to America and eventually settled with his new wife, Mary Clark, in the Genesee Valley. There, in 1854, they purchased the mill. Gilbert's experience in England and America made him an expert and efficient miller, and Gilbert's Mill became known to farmers and consumers throughout the valley. Gilbert died in 1888 and, following his death, two of his sons succeeded in the ownership of the property. Having helped in the mill from boyhood, they carried on the business as the "Gilbert Brothers" until after the turn of the century.

The 28-foot waterwheel in its stone well was housed inside the mill, protected from the winter, with an underground stone tunnel used to return water to the small stream. The wheel was fed by water diverted through a raceway from a millpond formed by damming the spring-fed Rock Bottom Creek.

The façade of Gilbert Mill still has its original doors, windows, and openings. The Dutch door is still the way in for visitors. The inward-swinging loading door above and the windows are protected by thermopane glass. In the left foreground is a millstone spindle that missed the scrap drive.

Although no flour has been ground since the 1820s, grandson George Gilbert, an expert mechanic and millwright, used the mill to grind animal feed until 1944, when the waterwheel was sold for scrap metal during World War II. The mill was then abandoned.

Interior designer Kenneth C. Gernold purchased the mill in 1953 from the last surviving Gilbert family member. He then began his mission of restoration and preservation. There was no chance of reestablishing operation of the mill since the old stone dam had been demolished and the water rights and sluiceway had been given to the Town of Avon. Neglected for more than forty years, the building was a ruin with leaking roofs, peeling clapboards, crumbling foundations, and missing windows.

The mill was converted into a dwelling place. The 42-foot-long, square hand-hewn beams, pegged and fitted together to withstand the vibrations of the mill, are still predominant in the great rooms. Remnants of the milling operation that remained were kept, and grain chutes still jut down from their original positions between the heavy timbers. In 1995, the Landmark Society of Western New York presented Gernold with an award for his work and determination in restoring and preserving the only remaining gristmill in the Genesee Valley.

The lower, stone-built level of the mill with the original windows, and Dutch door complete with its latch.

Two views of the internal stone foundations that once supported the internal, 28-foot waterwheel. Above is the waterwheel pit. The open end illuminates the area that was once a stone wall, which collapsed when the wheel was ripped out for a World War I scrap drive. On the right is another view of the wheel pit looking through from the main room. The openings allowed for the wheel axle and gears.

The milling floor is now the main living area. The walls and ceiling stay unpainted and virtually untouched. Some of the many openings for chutes and shafts have been left as found. The stone hoops, hopper, horse, and the crane remain as found. The real change is unseen; most of the original floor had fallen through or disappeared and had to be rebuilt.

Kenneth Gernold kept what was left in the mill after its
abandonment: chutes, elevators, parts of sifting machinery
all remain on their original levels as reminders of the mill's
history. The original dormer was once the only fenestration
on the bin floor: there were two, but the miller removed one
to reduce taxes. The one shown is now filled by a window
rescued from a demolished church in Rochester. The wheat-
sheaf design repeats the story of the mill's purpose. Massive
beams support parts of a dust collector.

Along a stretch of the Silvermine River, in southern Connecticut, there were a dozen mills almost in sight of each other. The proliferation was not because of any truth in the rumor that silver had been found, but because of the economic value water power could bring to the adjoining towns of Norwalk and New Canaan. The small mills included tanning works, sawmills, and spool works. Artists began to settle in the area in the 1900s and the community they established is the heart of Silvermine today.

Sculptor Solon Borglum was one of the first; his brother, Guston, carved the presidents' faces on Mount Rushmore. Among the group who gathered frequently was landscape painter Frank Townsend Hutchens, who bought Sammy Rider's 150-year-old mill in 1912 because of its location and potential as a home site. Today, close to 240 years old, the building had been a cotton- batting-mill, then a tobacco ware-house. During the first Colonial revival it turned out knobs for bureaus and highboys. It then evolved into a saw-mill. But when Hutchens' artist eye was drawn to the interior timbers, he wanted to keep the building intact. Mr. Rider had plans for another mill upstream and was helpful with his advice to the artist and his architect, imparting especially his knowledge of the ways of the river for their plans to get running water inside the mill.

To be safe to live in, the mill had to meet the threat of springtime floods. The basement had to be above any possible flooding, so the building had to be raised. When complete, the mill was ready for the rest of the twentieth century, with modern conveniences, servants' quarters, and a billiard room; a separate building, a few yards away, became Mr. Hutchens' studio.

A *view upstream from the millrace.*

221

Hutchens' original thoughts on how to "improve" the mill are still there today. He acquired two cast-iron balconies from New Orleans to face downstream and added sleeping porches. The mill was squeezed between the river and the road but at right angles, so all subsequent additions and remodeling have been to turn the aspect of the building to look out and over the river. In Sammy Rider's day there were different, more practical concerns.

After eighty years as a house, important changes were needed. The present owner called upon Richard Bergmann, an architect with expertise in historic preservation and adaptive reuse, to help. In spite of the changes over the years, there were no clear views of the spectacular river and the surrounding countryside from inside the house, the increased traffic noise and activity were affecting privacy, and there was a much-needed expansion for living space.

Bergmann designed additions in three separate areas. The smaller one, coming out of the original house and turned at an angle orienting the front door to the entry gate, is the new front entrance/foyer. Previously, guests had difficulty finding the front door. The second addition, also on the lower level facing the road, was where the architect cleverly incorporated a little-used porch by constructing outside the original building line.

The little-used porch.

A thirty-foot-long skylight over a six-foot-high stone wall washes the interior with light. The stone also acts as a buffer. This room is the library and expands the cramped living room. The south wall received a large area of glass and now reveals the millrace and the river downstream.

The stream side of the living room retains its original posts and main beams. The French doors open up to one of the iron balconies from New Orleans.

The largest addition was the expansion of the second floor, with a new sitting room/ guest room suite. The new windows on the north wall were carefully placed so that each pane framed a separate and distinct "landscape painting" and block any view from the road.

The second-floor sitting room looks out over the Silvermine River. The windows on the right bring in light, but their placement screens the interior from the outside.

A bedroom's old hand-hewn rafters reveal the oldest part of the building before it became a sawmill.

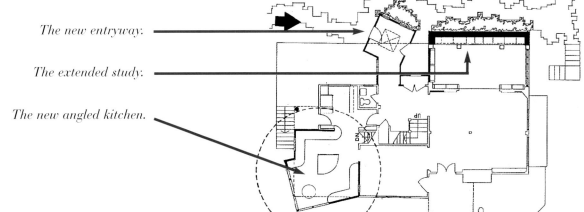

The new entryway.

The extended study.

The new angled kitchen.

More recently there was a fourth addition. The old kitchen was gutted, and new angled walls were cantilevered over the terrace to expand the breakfast seating area and to follow the line of the river, offering more fantastic views of the river and the upstream waterfall.

Now, in the new kitchen extension, the waterfall can be seen for the first time in its own frame.

Since this large stone Pennsylvania mill stopped working it has a had a novel adaptive use. With all the machinery intact, it is now called The Knittery, and welcomes both customers for the clothing and visitors who are just interested in the mill.

Cley Windmill dates from the early nineteenth century and is a well-known landmark on the North Norfolk Coast. The mill itself has been converted into a small guest house of great character and charm, and the old stables and boat sheds transformed into self-catering accommodation.

The mill stands on the north side of the village in a position of great peace and beauty. It overlooks Blakeney Harbor, the salt marshes, and Cley Bird Sanctuary.

The new mill was first offered for sale in the *Norfolk Chronicle* on June 26, 1819, and passed through several hands during the next hundred years. The best known of the millers was Steven Barnabas Burroughs, who worked in and owned the mill from 1840 to 1919, after which it fell into disrepair. In 1921 it was bought by Sarah Maria Wilson and converted into a holiday home. The conversion involved removing most of the working parts and fixing the cap and sails. The old stones, used for grinding the flour, were set into the ground nearby and the warehouses were converted into stables and boat sheds.

In 1953 the sea returned to Cley, which suffered its worst flooding in four hundred years. The mill stood firm but much of the furniture was damaged or washed away. A sea wall was built around the remainder of the village. In 1961 the fan bearings ran dry; before they were eased the resulting noise was heard all over the village for several days. In 1979 the mill passed to Charles Blount, and in 1983 it was renovated and converted into its present form.

The conversion of the mill in the 1920s and the recent improvements have resulted in a unique home combining comfort with character. The ground-floor room includes a magnificent circular sitting room where family paintings adorn the walls and antique furniture nestles comfortably around a roaring open fire. The beamed dining room has a warm and friendly atmosphere. The upstairs room and galleries have magnificent views over the marshes, Blakeney Harbor, and the sea.

Weybourne Mill dates from about 1850 and ended its working days
during the Great War. At the end of the 1920s it was the residence of
J. Sydney Brocklesby, an architect who was part of the Arts and Crafts
movement at the beginning of the century. Very recently the mill has
undergone a careful and sensitive restoration by a couple who, after
studying both the history of the mill and the career of its onetime
resident artist/architect, have incorporated the elements of both
with great harmony.

By the 1960s, the buildings were much altered and the mill had become
a mixture of styles. Also, as today's owners surveyed the mill they discovered that it was subsiding and likely to collapse in a couple of years.
Their plan was to both restore the historic mill tower and the Brocklesby
elements, adding an Arts and Crafts feel to what was to become a home,
an office, and a place to make music.

The fusion of the two structures shows up well in the restoration, with local cobbled finish and red bricks.

Brocklesby was attracted to the mill at the edge of the North Sea by the magnificent views in all directions. He turned it into a family vacation home, enlarging the residence by converting the mill tower floors into rooms. Important personal statements by the architect were the high and narrow framed windows on what was the main, second-level living floor, chosen for its outlook.

A new staircase was needed, and the owners arrived at a design that they felt complemented Brocklesby's work. The distinctive long windows had rotten frames at the base and were rebuilt from the bottom. The brickwork of the tower that joined the inside of the mill house had been painted white; and the curved wall was returned to its natural color, exposing an earlier roofline which remains to tell its story. In the right foreground is the original millpost from earlier times when a post mill stood on this site.

The "Brocklesby" windows.

A detail of the entry area.

A bedroom in the tower.

The music room below.

Jack is a handsome English mill with a large, white beehive cap, measuring sixteen-feet-in diameter inside topped by a ball finial. From the stage here, gained through a neat storm door in the back of the cap, there is an impressive view over Wolstonbury Hill to the west and the Weald beyond Clayton Village four hundred feet below. Jack is the companion to Jill (page 129) and is understood to have been built in 1866 and stopped working in 1907.

Jack's original sweeps, a fine set of double-shuttered patents, disappeared by 1973. Those we see today are courtesy of a film company making a Michael Caine movie, *The Black Windmill*, who paid a millwright to erect them.

Jack's cap has proven to be extremely weathertight with double-shingled ash lapping.

E.A. Martin, an archaeologist, then spent summers at the mill between 1908 and 1910. *The Windmills of Sussex* gives an account of his experiences there: "At this time Mr. Martin was in residence and tells us of his stay in his book *Life in a Sussex Windmill*. He actually lived in the first two floors and the adjoining roundhouse of the original Duncton post mill. Romantic though it may seem, he gives a different picture of life in the mill. The furnishing was something of a problem, as can be imagined, the carpets and fittings of a twelve-foot-square room are rather lost in one twenty feet or so in diameter with an iron pillar in the center. The pictures had to be pinned back to the sloping walls, and Mr. Martin recalled with amusement how, when opening the door on a windy day, every loose object skated and whirled around the room. Not so amusing were the insects and mice, which inhabited the mill at night, and the groan and clank of the cap as the fan kept the weatherbeaten sweeps into the wind. Passersby would call upon him after peering through the window and insist that this was their right, and that he should serve teas. I am sure that the spirit of the Downs more than compensated for these troubles, for he seemed happy to be here and did, in fact, make several archaeological studies during his stay."

The well-worn stairs inside the brick wall.

In 1911 the mill was occupied by the Anson family, who stayed for over forty years. Mrs. Anson's father and her husband had been naval officers. In their memory, she had the millstone floor fitted out as chapel in memory of her seafaring menfolk.

The sign taped to the stone hoop says "Don't touch the product," because this Tuscan gristmill receives occasional visitors unfamiliar with the etiquette of milling.

As an illustration for a book about the family mill as the center of life, this is the most enduring. The Grifonis have continued the tradition since 1696, when they engraved the date on the door lintel. They were not the first here; it was a communal mill in the 1400's before the Grifonis bought it. Today, it is run by two young brothers, Andrea and Fabrizio Grifoni, who supply wheat flour from a run of two stones to bakeries in the Cortona region. Another two stones grind corn, *granturco* for polenta, and dried chestnuts to make *farina dolce, or* sweet flour.

Apart from the small hoppers and stainless-steel fittings, the whirring rhythms and the clicking sounds of the turbine-driven stones and bolter are familiar to anyone who has been lucky enough to visit a country mill at work.

Glossary

AIR BRAKES Longitudinal boards in outer end of leading edge of a sail, actuated by shutter mechanism to open and break up airflow in heavy gusts.

APRON Arc of stone or wood placed behind a pitch back or breast shot waterwheel to prevent water from spilling from the buckets of the waterwheel before arriving at the lowest point of the fall.

ARMS Spokes extending from the main shaft of a water-wheel, which in turn support the shrouding or rims of the wheel, or spokes of a large gear wheel.

BACK EDGE Straight "back" edge opposite the grinding edge of a millstone furrow. It is also called the holding edge.

BACK STAYS Supporting bars across the back of the sail.

BACKWINDED Mill caught by wind when the sails are not facing the wind.

BAILS Large iron tongs suspended from a crane, used to lift off the upper stone of a pair for dressing or to make other adjustments to the stones.

BALANCE RYND Curved iron bar that crosses the eye of the runner millstone, fitting into slots or pockets on either side. Also called millstone bridge or crossbar.

BEARD Decorated board behind the canister on the cap of Dutch mills.

BEDSTONE Lower of a pair of millstones, which remains stationary.

BEEHIVE CAP Southern English name for a domed cap on a windmill.

BIG WHEEL See master face wheel.

BILLS Wedge-shaped pieces of metal used for chipping (dressing) millstones.

BINS Storage containers for grain, usually on the upper floor of a mill, from which grain can be fed into millstone hoppers.

BIST Cushion usually made of a partly filled sack of meal or bran, used as a cushion by a worker (millstone dresser) when dressing the millstones.

BLADES Panels attached to a shaft to harness water or wind power. Also called vanes.

BLUE STONE See Cullin stones.

BOLTER Machine used to sift flour into lots of different textures or degrees of fineness.

BOLTING CLOTH Cloth of varying closeness of weave used to sift flour by texture and size. The cloth used is often silk.

BRAKE Wooden or iron brake shoe encircling a brake wheel.

BRAKE WHEEL The primary gear wheel in a windmill, which is attached to the windshaft.

BRAN Outer coating of a grain of wheat, rye, barley, or corn.

BREAST Supports the head bearing of the windshaft at the front of a windmill.

BREAST SHOT WATERWHEEL Waterwheel powered by a head of water striking the wheel at the point from one-third to two-thirds the height of the wheel, causing the wheel to revolve in a direction opposite that of the flow of the water in the sluice way or millrace.

BRIDGE Metal bar cemented into eye of runner stone to act as bearing for the top of the spindle.

BRIDGE TREE Lever beam that carries the lower end of the spindle and thus bears the weight of the runner stone.

BUCK The whole body of a post mill above the trestle, which revolves as the mill is winded.

BUCKETS The blades or enclosures formed by blades around the rim of a waterwheel, against which or into which the water flows. They are called floats or paddles when they are a single flat blade or surface, and elbow buckets or buckets if they are formed from a front plate or blade and a bottom plate or bucket.

CANISTER Where the stocks of a windmill are attached.

CANT POSTS Main corner posts of a smock mill.

CAP Movable top section of tower or smock mill.

CHAIN WHEEL Wheel turned by means of an endless chain. For winding mill or for working striking gear.

CLOTH SAILS Sails with a wooden framework covered by cloth.

COLOGNE STONES See Cullin stones.

COMMON SAILS Cloth sails.

COMMON TOLL Toll exacted as payment for grinding corn.

CONTROL GATE Gate at the end of the flume or sluice box nearest to the waterwheel, used to control the flow of water from the box to the wheel. Also called a shut.

CRACKS Fine lines cut into the face or land of a millstone in the areas between the furrows.

CROSS TREES Large horizontal beams, the ends of which rest on masonry or brick piers at the base of the trestle on a post mill, and which carry the weight of the whole structure via the quarter bars.

CROWN WHEEL Horizontal gear wheel engaging with the vertical gear wheel.

CULLIN STONES German millstones of dark bluish-gray lava with even pores. The name is a corruption of Koln, the German name for the city called Cologne.

CUSTOM MILL Small milling operation that ground flour and meal to satisfy the needs of a local community. The miller was paid with a percentage of the ground meal.

DAMSEL A contraption above the bridge on under-driven stones, which causes the shoe to vibrate, shaking grain down into the eye.

DRESS The layout or pattern of furrows on a millstone. Also used with respect to flour to mean "sift."

DRESSER Person who works on the millstone furrows or cracking. Also the machine that bolts or sifts flour, as in dresser or dressing machine.

DRESSING Process of cutting grooves (cracks or furrows) into the face of the millstone.

EDGE MILL Mill in which the stones run on their edges.

EYE Hole in the center of the runner stone through which grain passes into the middle of the two stones.

FACE GEAR Gear wheel with cogs mortised into its face, usually used in conjunction with a lantern pinion.

FAN STAGING A platfom of the fan mechanism at the top of a tower or smock mill.

FANTAIL Small, secondary windmill geared to turn the mill to face the wind.

FEED SHOE Guides grain from hopper into eye of stone.

FINIAL Pointed top of an ogee cap, with a knob on it.

FLOUR DRESSER Machine for separating flour from the rest of the meal.

FLUME Trough or channel that carries water from the head race to the point where the water strikes or enters the waterwheel. Also called sluiceway, sluice box, or lade.

FLY TACKLE Another name for a fantail.

FRENCH BURRS Prized millstones from France, made of small blocks of quartz fitted together.

FURROW Groove cut into the grinding surface or land of the millstone.

FURROWING STICK Wooden stick or straight edge used to mark out the line of the furrow used in dressing the millstones.

GRAIN HOPPER Hopper above the vat which holds the grain to be milled.

GREAT SPUR WHEEL Mounted near the bottom of the upright shaft, it meshes with the stone nuts to drive the millstones.

GREATER FACE WHEEL See master face wheel.

GRISTMILL Mill for the grinding of grain, principally wheat or corn.

HEAD (OF WATER) Difference in level between water entering the waterwheel and that leaving the waterwheel. Also called fall (of water).

HEAD RACE Channel that conveys water from the dam or millpond to the flume, sluice box, or directly to the waterwheel.

HOLLOW POST MILL Post mill in which the drive passes down through the center of the post to the gearing at the bottom.

HOOP See stone case or vat.

HOPPER Open-topped container, tapered to feed grain into the millstones.

HORSE Wooden framework on top of the millstone case or cover, which holds the hopper, shoe, and (the top end of the) damsel in position.

HURST FRAME Timber framework that supports the millstones and gears. It is mounted on a separate and independent foundation from the mill so the vibration of the machinery does not bring down the mill around it.

JACK STICK See quill stick and trammel.

LANDS High parts of pattern on the grinding surfaces of millstones.

LANTERN PINION Pinion gear consisting of round staves or rungs mortised between two discs, used either as a wallower, or as a millstone pinion or nut.

LEADER BOARDS Longitudinal boards on the front or leading edge of a sail.

MACE Jaws at top of spindle which slot over the bridge, thus providing the drive to the runner stone.

MAIN POST Upright post on which a post mill revolves.

MAIN SHAFT Vertical shaft from wallower to spur wheel.

MASTER FACE WHEEL Face wheel mounted on the waterwheel shaft in countergearing; used to transfer power to the lay shafts via lantern pinions. Also called greater face wheel or big wheel.

A hurst frame

MIDDLINGS Coarsest part of the wheat meal ground by a mill; the last product excepting the bran remaining after finer grades of flour are sifted out in the bolting process.

MILLER'S TOLL Portion of ground meal retained by the miller as payment for his services.

MILLPOND Body of water, usually created by the construction of a dam, which serves as a source of water for the water wheel.

MORTISE WHEEL Iron wheel with wooden cogs mortised into it.

NECK BEARING Front bearing that supports the windshaft.

OGEE CAP Domed cap with reverse curve at the top and a more or less pointed finial culminating in a knob.

OPEN STONES Coarse, uncut millstones.

OVERSHOT WATERWHEEL Waterwheel powered by a head of water striking the wheel just behind its vertical center, or just forward its vertical center at its highest point of rotation.

PAINT STAFF See wood proof.

PATENT SAILS Shuttered sails linked through a spider to an automatic opening and shutting mechanism.

PIT WHEEL Large face gear wheel mounted on the waterwheel shaft and located in a pit or gear pit.

PITCH BACK WATERWHEEL Waterwheel powered by a head of water striking the waterwheel at or just behind its highest point, causing the waterwheel to "pitch back," or revolve in a direction opposite to that of the flow of water in the sluice box or sluiceway.

POLL END Large cast-iron socket on the end of the windshaft through which the stocks pass.

POST MILL The entire body of the mill turns on a center post.

PROOF STAFF Metal straight edge or gage used to check the true of a paint staff.

QUARTER A MILL To turn it slightly off the wind to slow it down.

QUERN Hand-operated mills used for grinding corn before the invention of water mills and windmills.

QUILL STICK Flat piece of wood with a hole to accommodate a feather quill in one end, and a square hole on the other that fits onto the millstone spindle. It is used to test the millstone spindle for true, upright running. Also called jack stick, tram stick, and trammel.

RADDLE Mixture of red oxide or lampblack powder and water, used on a paint staff. The material will mark the high spots on a millstone.

ROLLER MILL Mill with grooved rollers.

ROUNDHOUSE Walled and roofed-in trestle part of a post mill, made to provide storage space for grain, etc.

RUNNER (MILL) STONE Upper, moving millstone in a pair of millstones.

RYND (RIND) Crossbar containing the bearing on which the upper runner stone of a pair of millstones rests and is balanced.

SACK HOIST Method of hoisting sacks or barrels vertically in a mill using a gear-driven system or a windlass barrel hoist system.

SCOOP WHEEL Vertical cast-iron wheel with paddles or scoops, which lifts the water from one level to another.

SHAKER ARM Arm attached to shoe, which contacts damsel.

SHOE Moving trough leading from hopper to the eye, which feeds the grain to the millstones.

SHUTTERS Movable vanes of springs and patent sails, which open and close to present a working surface to the wind.

SICKLE DRESS Form of millstone dress using a series of semicircular furrows of the same radius as the millstones. Also called circular furrow dress. This is the most common millstone dress used on Rhine stones.

SILK MACHINE Flour dresser with a silk sleeve.

SILKS See bolting cloth.

SKIRT Outer edge of the grinding surface of a millstone.

SILLS Horizontal timber plates on top of base walls of a smock mill to carry cant posts and framing.

SKIRT Outer section of millstones.

SLUICE Wooden box that is held together by a series of wooden frames. It is often mounted on wooden piers, and carries water over valleys to maintain the height of the water from its source to the waterwheel.

SMOCK MILL Wooden-framed, many-sided mill, clad with wood or thatch, with a movable cap. Some are built on a stone or brick base.

SPIDER Iron cross on end of striking rod, linked to bell cranks and levers of striking gear.

SPINDLE Bar carrying stone nut, which passes up through millstones to engage with the bridge and mace and carry the runner stone.

SPINDLE The shaft on which the runner millstone rotates.

SPRING-LOADED SHUTTERS Shutters of spring sails.

SPRING SAIL Sail with shutters linked to a spring. The tension of which has to be set manually on each sail so that the shutters will open and close according to wind strength.

STOCKS The main bars that cross through the top of the windshaft and support the sails.

STONE DRESSER A person who resharpens or dresses millstones.

STONE CASE Circular wooden enclosure around a pair of millstones. Also called casing, hoop, husk, tun, and vat.

STONE NUTS Pinion wheels mounted on a spindle or quant which are moved into gear with the great spur wheel to drive the millstones.

STRIKING ROD Rod that links spider to adjusting mechanism of a patent sail by passing down through the hollow windshaft and out through its lower end.

SWEEPS Another term for sails.

TAILPOLE Long beam attached to the back of an early windmill by which it can be turned into the wind.

TAILRACE Lower portion of a millrace or channel. It is the section that returns water to the millstream after is has flowed through the waterwheel.

TENTERING Process of adjusting the distance between the upper and lower millstones.

TOWER MILL Mill built of brick or stone with a movable cap.

TRESTLE The whole of the support system of a post mill.

TUB MILL Water mill with a horizontal wheel enclosed to its full depth with a wooden casing or open top and a bottom tub.

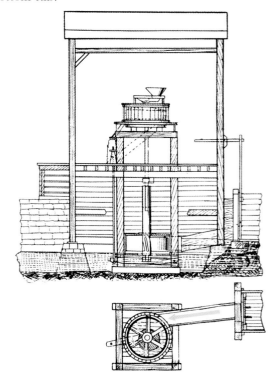

TUN See stone case.

TUN See vat.

UNDERDRIFT Stone driven from below.

UNDERSHOT WATERWHEEL Waterwheel powered by a head of water striking the wheel at the point near the bottom of the wheel, causing the wheel to revolve in the direction opposite that of the flow of water in the sluice box or millrace.

VANES Sails of a fantail or shutters of patent sails.

VARYING PITCH Twist from one end of the sail to the other. Sail bars are set on whips at a progressively greater angle from tip to heel of sail.

VAT See stone case.

WALLOWER The first driven wheel of a mill.

WHIPS Long bars attached to the front of the stocks which carry the sail bars, shutters, etc.

WINDED Turned to face the wind.

WINDING GEAR Tailpole or fantail for turning into the wind.

WINDSHAFT Axle on which the sails are mounted.

WOOD PROOF Wooden level for checking surface of millstones.

252

Acknowledgments

The mill lovers favorite, *The Young Millwright and Miller's Guide* is not an easy read. However revolutionary, it is after all, a tradesman's handbook, full of gudgeons, scantling, rynds, and rublings that sends non-millers to serious unabridged dictionaries. Enough terms, words and metaphors have come from a mill to fill a book longer than this one. In fact, I have learned that a 3,000 word glossary in English is currently being prepared for publication.
The short glossary, included here, covers what we have seen in this book and adds some descriptions that may help in further reading.

First of all, I would like to thank the fellow members of the Society for the Preservation of Old Mills who I have met and corresponded with. From published sources, The Society for the Preservation of Old Mills' publication, *Old Mill News*, with its erudite and enthusiastic contributions from millers, millwrights and mill restorers, has been the best source of all. Society members are busy recording, measuring, and sharing their discoveries of old mill sites and continue the campaign to spread the news about old mills.

I am grateful to all those listed below who have have helped me:

Stephen Kindig, who patiently answered my questions on milling and directed me towards examples of historic mills that are in the process of being sympathetically restored and preserved to work again; Ted Hazen, who allowed me to quote from his work and whose interests and activities in mills and millwrighting is exemplified on his website, Pond Lily Mill Restorations; Sandra Wittman for her work and knowledge on windmills; and Denny Plowman for some old press cuttings on milling life.

Alan Bately; Ed Behr; Sandra and Richard Bergmann; Roy Berry; Art and Donna Bert; Broads Authority, How Hill Trust; Hank Browne; Cley Windmill; Alisha Cole, Kansas City Museum, Parks and Recreation Department; Colvin Run Mill Historic Site; Rick Dixon; Ronnie Dodd; Paul Drumm, III; Stephen Earl, County Hall, Norwich; Essex County Council Planning Department; Amanda Evans, Bournemouth Art Institute; Nick Farris; John Fowle, The National Trust, Horsey Drainage Windpump; The French and Pickering Creeks Association Conservation Trust, Mrs. Samuel W. Morris; Kenneth Gernold; Sidney Halma, Catawba County Historical Association; Floyd Harwood; John Hubbard; Roy S. Hubbs; Dawn Kehrer; Anne Korzeniewski; Nancy Landis; Jane and John Lovett; Mason Maddox; Frank and Marjorie Martin; R.G. Martin; Norfolk County Council Planning Department; Norfolk Windmills Trust; Deborah O'Brien; Derek Ogden; Jim Owens; Vincent Pargeter; Dennis J. Pogue; Patrick G. Riley; Roberta Smith Riley; Sacrewell Water Mill, William Scott Abbott Trust; Eleanor Boggs Shoemaker; Steve Solley; Sussex Mills Group; The International Molinology Society (T.I.M.S.); Scott Tilton; Georgie and Jim Young; Sandra Wittman, Oakton Community College, Illinois.

Bibliography

Apling, Harry. Norfolk Corn Windmills. Norwich: Norfolk Windmills Trust, 1984.

Beedell, Suzanne. Windmills. New York, Charles Scribner's Sons, 1975.

Brooks, Ralph L. The Village That Slept Awhile. Indianapolis: Division of State Parks, 1965.

Freese, Stanley. Windmills and Millwrighting. London: Cambridge University Press, 1957.

Lord, Arthur C.. Water-Powered Grist Mills of Lancaster County, Pennsylvania. 1996

Norfolk County Council. Norfolk Windmills. Norwich: Norfolk County Council, 1995.

Pinney, R. C. Sussex Windmills and their Restoration. Brighton: Sussex Industrial Archaeology Society, 1999.

Woodbury, George. John Goffe's Mill. New York: W.W. Norton & Company, Inc., 1948.

Zimiles, Martha & Murray. Early American Mills. New York: Bramhall House, 1973.

Photo Credits